THEOSOPHY:
The Path of the Mystic

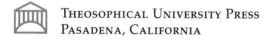 THEOSOPHICAL UNIVERSITY PRESS
PASADENA, CALIFORNIA

Katherine Tingley

THEOSOPHY:
The Path of the Mystic

Links for Your Own Forging

Compiled by Grace Green Knoche

Theosophical University Press
Post Office Box C
Pasadena, California 91109-7107
1995

Library of Congress Cataloging-in-Publication Data

Tingley, Katherine Augusta Westcott, 1847–1929
    Theosophy, the path of the mystic : links for your own forging /
Katherine Tingley ; compiled by Grace Green Knoche. — 3d and rev.
ed. — Pasadena, Calif. : Theosophical University Press, c1977.
    x, 159 p. ; 20 cm.
    ISBN 0-911500-33-2 (alk. paper)
    ISBN 0-911500-34-0 (alk. paper) pbk
    1. Theosophy.   I. Knoche, Grace Green, comp. II. Title.
BP565.T5   1977   147   77-82604
                                             MARC
Library of Congress   78₍7910₎

Printed at Theosophical University Press
Pasadena, California

CONTENTS

Foreword   vii

I   What Is Theosophy?   1

II   The Great Discovery   15

III   The Path of the Mystic   39

IV   Teacher and Student   61

V   The Heart-cry of the World   81

VI   The Family and the Home   113

VII   Ideals and the Child   137

Who was Katherine Tingley? The truly faithful evaluation of a life is not easily come by, for who can know the inner motivation of another, the wellspring of aspiration that moves to thought and deed? That Katherine Tingley was a "lover of mankind," a philanthropist in the most profound meaning of the word, is without question, for her entire life was an outpouring of compassion for all who suffer.

Born in 1847 in Newbury, Massachusetts, close to the Merrimac she loved so well, Catharine Augusta Westcott was reared in an atmosphere of culture. But even as a child she was haunted by the poverty and misery of the immigrants who came to work the land, by the gaunt and hopeless faces of prisoners and, in her early teens, by the "vileness and terror of war." In 1861, shortly after the outbreak of hostilities between the States, her father's regiment was stationed in Virginia, and the conditions she and her brother witnessed day after day so affected the sensitive girl that one night she could stand it no longer and stole out with her old nurse to tend the wounds of the returning soldiers, giving what comfort she could.

A lonely child, she would spend long hours under

the giant oaks and pines on the river's edge, dreaming dreams. Though her family loved her, they did not understand her — with the exception of her maternal grandfather, a mystic and Freemason. Always he listened, confident that one day she would realize her vision of building a "city" in the Golden West.

The years were to bring much personal sorrow, but this only deepened her sympathies for the downtrodden, and strengthened her determination to do something practical, something that would eradicate the *causes* of their appalling plight. As she had no explanation for the cruel inequities she met with at every turn, she worked all the harder to relieve what distress she could. In the early 1890s she organized a Women's Emergency Relief Association in New York and also, in one of the worst slum areas on the Eastside of the city, a Do-Good Mission.

One morning, when she had turned the Mission into a temporary relief station for feeding and clothing the families of destitute strikers, she noticed on the far edge of the crowd a gentleman observing her. When she tried to contact him, thinking that possibly he also was in need, he was gone. A day or so later, he presented his card at her home: William Q. Judge. They talked, and when he told her, "your work is Theosophy," she replied that the word meant little to her — "I only know that humanity needs broader views of life."

She was cautious, as too many times she had been disappointed. But the teachings of reincarnation and karma, and that man is inherently divine and not "born in sin," had taken hold, and soon she knew that here was the hope and promise she had longed for; here was a philosophy which, if practiced, could lighten the burdens of "poor, storm-tossed humanity."

Katherine Tingley and William Q. Judge became co-workers, and upon his death in March, 1896, she succeeded him as head of the Theosophical Society. The next month at the Annual Convention of American theosophists held at Madison Square Garden, New York, her intent to establish an educational center that would restore a knowledge of the sacred mysteries of antiquity was revealed. By June, capacity crowds at Boston and New York learned of her world-tour to bring the message of theosophy to all classes: a message of hope, of another chance, of the dignity of every human being, and of brotherhood and peace. These were the themes she would reiterate in nearly every public lecture until her passing in Sweden thirty-three years later.

The Rāja-Yoga School, Academy and College at Point Loma, California, was Katherine Tingley's most noted humanitarian achievement. This was the fulfillment of her long-held dream of children, almost from infancy, being taught music, drama, and the arts as an intrinsic part of character building. A life of service and sharing was regarded as the natural expression of the balanced individual.

In retrospect, while her school no longer exists, the ideals she projected with incredible genius live into the future — seeding the thought-consciousness of the world with the vision of a new type of civilization in which all the faculties, physical, mental-emotional, and spiritual, would develop in harmony.

Far-reaching and significant as Katherine Tingley's educational activities were, in Cuba, Britain, Sweden and America, they constituted only a portion of the responsibilities she carried as international leader of a worldwide Theosophical Society. Not least of these was the expansion of the printing and publishing facilities to meet the growing demand for theosophical books and magazines. To her, theosophy never became "a system of sterile thought," but remained always "a light, a teacher, a companion, ever calling to compassionate action, ever urging to higher things." This was the keynote of her life mission, as it is of the present volume.

Theosophy: The Path of the Mystic is the quintessence of the theosophic wisdom that Katherine Tingley imbodied in letters, private group sessions, in talks with prisoners, students and faculty, as well as in public lectures delivered all across America and throughout the world. The book is not a text; rather it is a mosaic of suggestions and hints for daily living, with the appeal always to the higher, altruistic side of the nature, never to the lower, personal self. In the words of the compiler, Grace Green Knoche (1871–1962), a long-time student under Katherine Tingley, it is "for the seeker, the inquirer, the mystic; for those who have touched the great problem of sorrow and would gladly make their lives count in service to their fellows if they could only find the way."

Originally published in 1922, *Theosophy: The Path of the Mystic* was well received, and also appeared in several European languages, but for years it has been unavailable. It is now reissued with minimal editing, in the conviction that the message of this great esotericist speaks directly to the soul, to the inward yearning of every man and woman for assurance that there *is* a compassionate purpose to life; that there *is* a path, and that all of us can find it in our everyday lives if we dare to bring forth the divinely human qualities that are innately ours.

GRACE F. KNOCHE

Pasadena, California
July 6, 1977

Like as a bird cleaves the eternal ether, so the mystic advances on a path not ordinarily manifest.

— WILLIAM Q. JUDGE

What is Theosophy?

I

The Wisdom-Religion of the Ages

HE in whom the soul is ever manifest — he is the true mystic, and to him theosophy is no system of sterile thought but a light, a teacher, a companion, ever calling to compassionate action, ever urging to higher things.

Think of theosophy not so much as a body of philosophic or other teaching, but as the highest law of conduct, which is the enacted expression of divine love or compassion.

It will bring something to you that can never pass away: the consciousness of your divine, your inner self; a conviction of your inherent power to conserve your energy along the highest spiritual lines. For man cannot find his true place in the great scheme of human life until he has ennobled and enriched his nature with the consciousness of his divinity. That is what theosophy means; that is its message; and it is a beautiful one to those who can throw aside fear and prejudice and truly interpret its meaning.

New in its presentation, but old as the ages in its meaning, theosophy was once the universal religion of mankind, and is destined to be the universal religion of the future. Even now its great principles are permeating thought and action everywhere, and everywhere the most advanced minds are looking forward to the ideal of a universal religion as humanity's one hope.

Those who long to serve humanity should study its teachings, if for nothing else than that they may learn to "know themselves"; that they may learn to know their children spiritually; that they may perceive the duality that exists in human nature as well as in life, thus becoming able to control the disruptive and lower elements, and encourage those which are noble, constructive and divine. For the despair and unrest of humanity, the unbalance and the injustices of life, stand at the door of our civilization, like living pictures, specters, their very presence pleading for a manifestation of the higher law.

But the one who essays to study theosophy must do his part. He cannot be fed with a spoon. There must be effort and humility, aspiration and love of virtue, and a willingness to be taught.

No teacher, however great, can teach until the pupil is ready to learn.

Theosophy does not offer spiritual instruction for money. Truth is not purchasable.

Were you to be told that just outside the door great minds were waiting to give you the secret of acquiring fabulous wealth, you would not stop for anything. Yet that which you would hope to gain belongs but to the perishable, fleeting, material side of life. Why not make as great an effort for the knowledge that will give you the secret of right living, reveal to you the mysteries of life?

There is in theosophy an optimism so magical, so inspiring, and so superb that I would I had the power to challenge the world with its sublime ideas. Had we the light of this inspiring, pulsating philosophy upon the affairs of our nations today, we should find an inner and higher expression of brotherhood. The force of it would touch and quicken the most indifferent minds;

it would bring the breath of life to those who, weighed down by their karma, are now but just half living — yes, men and nations both. It is this above all that the world needs.

Its teachings can bring hope to poor, storm-tossed humanity; this I affirm, and we have but to observe the general trend of human thought and effort to establish this as a fact. Antiquated theories of religion and life are being discredited, long-settled beliefs and customs are being abandoned, and there has risen in the world a great compelling force which is demonstrating the poverty of man's religious life.

Materialism and the merely intellectual view have carried man out upon a sea of unrest and dissatisfaction, while the real man, the divine man, has been ignored. As a result, the finer knowledge — which is right at hand if we could but perceive it, for it lies in the very being of man himself — is inactive and obscured, so that it is difficult even for thinking men and women to find their moorings. It is this very condition, however, that will finally open man's eyes.

Theosophy is the inner life in every religion. It is no new religion, but is as old as truth itself.

The Mission of Theosophy

The mission of the Theosophical Society is to bring men and women together as co-workers for a great and universal purpose; and the first step towards that end is to accentuate the fact that *man is divine*, and that to help create a nucleus of universal brotherhood, based on the divinity of man and the immortality of the soul, is the duty of every human being.

Its mission is to set aside errors, misconceptions, unbrotherliness and intolerance, and put love and trust, right action and the sweetness of truth in their place; to spread new ideas throughout the world for the benefit of those who most need them; to release the mind of man from prejudice and from fear, and human life from its digressions. Its mission is to bring the whole human family up to a standard of spiritual fore-sight, discrimination, intuition, right thought and right action, with a new and diviner conception of justice and of love. If men and women could work together as one great universal body towards this end, they would be creators of a new order of ages, a universal religion verily, and a true brotherhood of man.

My whole aim is to bring out the spiritual possi-bilities of the individual — individual effort towards higher things. That is the aim of theosophy: that each may come to know himself better, that there may be a spiritual rounding-out of the character and the life. If the individual can rise in the strength of his divine heritage, the power of his spiritual rights, then comes a clearing of the mind, a lifting of the veil that hides the truth.

Yet we never proselytize. We make no attempt to convert; for the philosophy declares that any attempt to force others to accept our thought or our views is an injustice to their true nature, their deeper self. We do not frighten, intimidate or discourage, nor do we implant fear. But we do appeal, and we do try by example to show to others the beauty of theosophy as a living power.

❖

A new hope, a new courage, is even now stirring the hearts of thousands. A message of love and brotherhood has gone out to the world. This is the keynote of the new age — *brotherhood*.

The principles of theosophy are worthless unless carried out in deeds. It is useless to pile up in the library of our intellectual life ideas upon ideas — and nothing more. The world is weighed down with mere intellectualism already. It must have something more, and that something more is the active, practical expression of those ideas, those spiritual principles, in every act of life.

Its teachings show man how to reason in a new way. They challenge one to seek a new viewpoint, to rise in the strength of the soul to heights of self-mastery never attained before. But not for self: in this time of agony and chaos there can be no thought of self.

In such endeavor the student finds the sacredness of the hour and the day. There is no time for compromise or for delay. The lazy, the indifferent, the selfish and the egotistical will not be interested along such lines of research; but one who is stirred by the simple conviction that he is immortal — not in some nebulous future life, but *here and now* — that man feels the touch of the divinity within.

Theosophy has above all the power to uplift. If mankind but understood and lived it, the whole human race would be freed, a solid foundation of mental and spiritual freedom would be established and the present

9

menacing and terrible conditions would disappear. It teaches that man weaves his own destiny and that he is, *to the extent of his knowledge and his will*, the master of it.

For humanity *is* divine! Were this divinity but realized, the godlike attributes of character would be so manifest in dignity and in strength that no words would be needed to tell us what real life is! We are making some progress, it is true; but we hear only six notes played. The seventh one is silent, and that silent, waiting note is the *divine* in human nature and in life.

Helena Petrovna Blavatsky

I never think of the teachings of theosophy without feeling surge up within me an intense, an affectionate, an infinite regard for the wonderful woman who brought them to the Western world — teachings far older than those of the Nazarene, and yet with all the beauty, charm and purity of new life. I feel that she must have passed through many schools of experience in many, many lives to gain the marvelous knowledge that she possessed, the self-sacrificing love for humanity that was hers, and the courage that sufficed to carry her through the suffering and persecution that came. She was as one who had been cleansed as by fire, who had passed through the travail of the soul.

When Madame Blavatsky came to the world with her message, she perceived the materialistic trend of human thought and life, and brought her treasures of truth that she might turn that trend to higher things. She came to simplify the problems of life. Her purpose was to set men thinking. Read *The Secret Doctrine, Isis Unveiled, The Key to Theosophy*, and *The Voice of the Silence* — you who are questioning as to the whence, the wherefore and the whither — and see if you do not find in them principles and truths that, could they be lived up to, would absolutely change the whole aspect of our civilization. She was indeed "humanity's friend."

How was it possible for this teacher to find her way into the heart-life of the world as she did, and leave on the screen of time that indescribable something that has never been fully uttered? We can perceive as yet but one or two aspects of it — and these according to our advancement. In her life she expressed the unutterable, the mystical, the truly unexpressed. She dwelt in

11

the soul-life and under the impress of the silence. She brought to the world lofty and colossal principles, whose meaning our children as the years pass will interpret better than we. She lifted the veil before the mysteries of life and destiny when she stepped forth on the outer plane with this magnificent and dignified philosophy.

H. P. Blavatsky has been libeled and obscured, as all spiritual reformers have been; but thousands who know her teachings and her life hail her as one of the benefactors of the age. We already find the ideals of theosophy permeating every department of thought.

Humanity is truly in the shadows; but in spite of retrogression, materialism and a selfishness that is extreme, the finer atmosphere of the world is even now surcharged with hope. Can we take the light and sunshine of this hope into our lives and forget the one to whose courage and sublime effort we owe all this — H. P. Blavatsky?

She left the world in its thought-life teeming with an urge for higher things, which only the few could understand. She was inspired beyond the knowing, and the great message which she brought, the mighty undertones and overtones of universal love, sounded by her in the silences, were part of the great universal plan. She was the messenger of years to come, the torchbearer of the age, the great transmitter of spiritual light to the future.

The Great Discovery

II

The Duality of Man's Nature

THERE is a great discovery which each must make for himself: that human nature is dual and that a battle is ever going on between the higher self and the lower, the angel and the demon in man. When the higher, immortal part dominates, there is knowledge and there is peace. When the lower rules, all the dark despairing elements of human life rush in upon the unguarded soul.

Man, in his inner nature, is a being with a divine inheritance and immeasurable possibilities of evolution.

This strange duality! And how do human weaknesses creep in? First of all we turn the key of selfishness in some closed door of the nature; then, before we know it, the door is open and in walks a stranger, an obsessive, potent force of evil, often with power enough to destroy the very being. No lens has as yet been made that can show you what this is, but it nevertheless exists. And the door of selfish desire once ajar, the incoming stranger is welcomed, entertained, permitted to enjoy the bounty of the intellectual life, permitted to sit in the very chamber of man's being, where only higher and splendid things should be.

This door may open in any of us, but know that it can never be shut, and kept shut, until our feet are planted on the eternal rock of knowledge and of trust, until we have the power — and absolutely know that we have it — to shut out the faintest tinge or touch or thought or vibration of anything that would mar the purity of that inner realm of mind that the soul works in and through.

In the name of justice and of karma I say: Woe be unto those who willfully entertain such visitors as these! Woe be unto those who dare to desecrate their own mind or touch the mind of another with anything but the loftiest, the noblest, the purest and the best!

Once the duality of human nature is admitted by science, our asylums will become great schools of study from which a deeper understanding and a larger compassion shall come. For without a study of the self *in its duality*, mental disorders cannot be understood. A volume could be written on this one line alone, and the half not then be told.

How wonderfully farseeing was that old teacher of bygone days who left us this injunction: MAN, KNOW THYSELF! That is the key to the whole situation. Let man take the first step boldly in honest self-examination, with a daring that stops before nothing that may impede his path, and he will find very soon that he has the key to wisdom and to the power which redeems. Discovered through his own efforts, by the law of self-directed evolution, this key will open before him the chambers of the self.

For when a man has the courage to analyze himself — his purposes, his motives, his very life; when he dares to compare the wrong things in his life with the right ones, in the spirit of a love for humanity sufficient to make him willing to lay down his life for it if need be, he will find the secret of living. This is what I mean when I say that we are ever being challenged — challenged by the better side of our natures to stand face to face with ourselves, to reach out in recognition to the divinity within. For this divinity, this knower,

19

this spiritual companion, is ever pleading to be listened to, ever waiting to be recognized, ever ready to help and serve that it may bring the whole nature of man to its standard of godlike perfection.

These two forces: the physical dominated by the spiritual, the mind illuminated by treasures of truth and inspiration from the higher self, these two, working together, will bring about results that are unbelievable. Nor will it take all eternity to bring about these things. The very atoms of our body can be touched by the fire of divine life and brought into harmony with the mind and soul, controlled as the master musician controls his instrument by the higher self.

For life is light and light is life, and the Christos-spirit is in everything in degree. Could we sit at the feet of the Law like little children, could we free our minds from misconceptions and learn from nature and listen to the Christos-voice within, what revelations would come to us! We should then be able to say: this is immortal and that is mortal; this belongs to the animal nature of man, and that to the spiritual. The power to do this is the power that we need, arousing us from the dead, so to speak, and bringing to us light and illumination.

20

Man's Two Companions

From the time that a vow is taken the disciple has ever with him two forces: two invisible companions formed of his own essence, one evil, one divine; the secretion or objectivation of the opposite poles of his own self-consciousness, they represent his good and evil angels, the Augoeides and its counterpart, each seeking to absorb his being. One of these in the end must prevail over the other, and one or the other is strengthened by every act and thought of his life. They are his higher and lower potentialities passing slowly into potency, as the energies (both good and evil) are awakened.

Our problem is to transfer more and more of ourselves to the real battlefield. That field is one that consists of the feelings and thoughts of men; therefore, by right feeling and thought is the battle maintained. Our strength lies in keeping positive; in holding a steady joy in our hearts; in a momentary meditation on all floating great ideas till we have seized them and made them ours; in a meditation with the imagination on the life of humanity in the future, and its grandeur; in dwelling on the conception of brotherhood.

21

Yet never can we reach that point of spiritual discernment until we have found within our own hearts
something new: a larger sympathy for all that lives,
and a broader, deeper, grander conception of human
life and the superb laws that govern it.

I think each is a focalization to a point of all the
good and all the evil elements to which we have given
conscious life in the past. At each moment, as we consciously incline toward good or evil, one or the other
feeds into and fills the mind. And it is obvious that the
point of connection with either is that failing or virtue
to which we are most inclined. However small a point,
it must, if encouraged, lead to and involve all the rest
on that side of the stores of our nature and the universe.
If this is true, it follows that to give our *conscious*
volitional encouragement and backing to any fault or
any failing, is *an immensely pregnant move downward.*

But if effort be continual, if no failures or falls
discourage the aspirant and are always followed "by as
many undaunted struggles upward," he has always the
help and counsel of the divine "daimon," the Warrior;
and victory, however far away, is certain. For this is
an unconquerable power, "eternal and sure," an actual

22

presence and inspiration, if we will but recognize it, having faith and faith and faith.

Why, then, it will be natural to ask, if this Warrior, fighting for us, is invincible, do we ever fail? It is lack of faith, unwontedness of resort to this place of energy, the habit of yielding to temptation without pause or thought, the nonrecognition by meditation of the duality of our nature.

Reconstruction and Duty

Reconstruction is the great keynote of effort at the present time, for it is a time of new things, new light, and very great help, if we invoke it.

The reconstruction of humanity! How shall we set about it? The first step, I hold, is to declare to man: *You are divine! There is within you soul-life, and if you* WILL *to bring out that life it will reveal to you the truth; it will make clear every step that you take. Greatest of all, it will reveal to you your duty.* For humanity at present is working largely on mistaken lines of duty.

Duty is misunderstood, as are justice and equity. Yet if we could free ourselves from the limitations of preconceived ideas — ideas that are literally riveted into the mind — we could move out into the free air of harmonious thought and action, and would know what duty is. The things we believed in yesterday we should believe in no longer; the false gods we have worshiped in our home life and the life of the nation, would vanish in the presence of the new light.

For the light is only waiting to be perceived. You need not go to India, nor wait for the touch of a swami's hand, in order to find that light. You can find it for yourselves, although since all have evolved differently, in different environments, under different conditions, and up to different points of understanding, one cannot say *when* or *how*. To establish a set rule for reformation would therefore be unwise. This we do know, however, that with the motive pure and the soul ever urging one upward, one moves forward naturally on lines of simple duty, and thus into the light of the higher nature and of truth.

❖

O ye men and women, children of the same Universal Mother as ourselves! Ye who were born as we

24

were born, who must die as we must die, and whose souls like ours belong to the Eternal: I call upon you to arise from your dreamy state and to see within yourselves that a new and brighter day has dawned for the human race.

This need not remain the age of darkness, nor need you wait until another age arrives before you can work at your best. It is only an age of darkness for those who cannot see the light, for the light itself has never faded and never will. It is yours if you will turn to it, live in it; yours today, this hour even, if you will hear what is said with ears that understand.

Arise then, fear nothing, and taking that which is your own and all men's, abide with it in peace for evermore!

❖

Wisdom comes not from the multiplication of spoken or written instructions; what you have is enough to last you a thousand years. Wisdom comes from the performance of duty, and in the silence, and only the silence expresses it.

25

Let us bring into life as an active, potent factor that knowledge which is not to be purchased, for it is only to be won by the surrender of the lower nature — the passionate, the selfish, the lustful nature — to the Christos-spirit, the god within. Then let us call forth this inner, divine self, that it may illuminate the mind and bring man to the heights of spiritual discernment, to knowledge of the higher self.

We shall never possess the courage that rightfully belongs to man as part of the divine law, until we know that *we are souls*, until we have opened new doors of experience in our lives, interpreting life according to this law and the higher knowledge of our being.

When with great effort a man has clarified his nature, when he can say: Get thee behind me, Satan! — then has he entered the path of self-development. Though his lower nature may meet him at every turn of the path, never can he fail if his purpose is pure. The godlike qualities of his higher nature are disciplining him, because he has said: It shall be so.

Greater than all Christ knew was the divine compassion that he felt; and it must have been when on the heights, sounding the harmonies of the soul in his compassion for humanity, that he looked into the future, beheld the divine possibilities of those who were to come, and said: Greater things than these shall ye do.

The mentality of man will never be fully developed until he has made his own the enlightenment that comes from soul-knowledge. And yet each holds this rare possession within his heart of hearts. It belongs to all men; they have but to claim their own.

Self-Study and Self-Control

Self-analysis, self-study, self-control: these are the divine, protective power, the golden keys to an understanding of the self. Oh, that we might realize what books of revelation are piled up on the shelves of our own lives!

Have you meditated on that higher self to which you aspire? This is the first step to an understanding of the real nature of the inner and outer man. It clarifies your whole being, unloading and separating from you

27

much that you have hitherto thought to be yourself, helping you to an understanding of the valuelessness of much that you have hitherto desired and perhaps thought necessary to your welfare or peace of mind; separating the chaff from the wheat in consciousness, conferring added power of insight into human nature, and discrimination in your dealings with men.

We are too slow in looking at these grave problems of human nature from the practical standpoint, too dilatory in our efforts to study them from analogy. Yet this is just what we must do if we are to go forward on the path of self-conquest and real helpfulness to others. We may talk about duality all day; but what does it avail if we do not apply our knowledge to the conditions of actual life?

It is in the mysterious chambers of the self, within the very atoms of the mind, that the little weakness, the little untruthfulness or disobedience, the all but unnoticed vice, take root and grow, marking the subtle beginnings of an evil that is worse than a crawling, venomous reptile ready to spring at your throat. This is a vivid picture, but we need it — to see things as they are.

28

To reconstruct mankind we must arouse more faith in the self. The spiritual failure becomes such because man has lost faith in himself. That is always the initial step. Then comes loss of faith in his friends, then in mankind as a whole, and soon he finds himself living in a strange house: the house of the lower nature.

It is an awful spectacle, the decay of a loyal nature. So little a bar seems to keep the poor, unhappy mind, fluttering through its delusions, from finding its own place of peace. But even these cases can help, if we study them and learn from them the two keynotes that mark our own duality: one inducing worry, the hot brain, misery, discordant overtones, self-justification, and again and again self-justification, an eternal harping on that; the other peace, love, joy, clear vision, work.

No one, thoroughly set in a wrong course, can ever be brought to a realization of that fact by words alone. Why? Because the lower nature is *there;* it is, for the time, master of the situation, master in the house of mind, inimical naturally to whatever would enable its victim to learn the truth.

We all know that the inner man is true, eternal, strong, pure, compassionate, just. The outer is too often weak, wavering, selfish; its energy arises out of desire and ambition. Yet it is the instrument which the soul, the inner, seeks to perfect in compassion. It is in this outer nature, usually physically dominated, that arises the common feeling of *I*, and it is to the blending of this with the real *I* that evolution tends.

Our consciousness is often a strangely self-gullible, dual entity. Victories are won first in thought; and the habit of substituting a good thought or picture that arouses compassion or any part of the spiritual nature, or a grander idea in any way going beyond the limited selfhood, for a selfish or personal or sensual one, is easily learned.

❖

To touch upon this moot question, so often raised by modern psychology, the question of habit: it is habit that makes or mars the character; but he who knows the dividing line between self-indulgence and self-control, has the key to habit and knows how to build aright.

I find myself thinking the same thing today that I did yesterday, holding the same ideal but with each day living closer to it, nearer to the warmth and glow of the real life. Soon habit is established, the habit of aspiration and self-control, the foundation of character.

Were this knowledge universal, there would open new paths in life. We should have no disharmonies, no war. We should have *religion itself* — religion that would lead us to see the beauties of nature in a new way, to study humanity in a new way, and to find the virtues of our brothers and cultivate them so understandingly and so generously that in time all hatred would disappear.

It is indeed time to think along these lines, for the spirit of hatred has passed so deeply into our natures — sucked in, so to speak, as the rain is sucked into the earth — that it will take no end of spiritual sunshine, no end of spiritual virility and splendid hope to bring us to a higher standard, with its promise of ultimate perfection.

The Higher and Lower Psychology

The duality of human nature is the great revelation in the realm of psychology. Were we to take John

31

Knox's old conception of the devil, and were we to intensify its fiendish nature and send it out into the world as a living personality, it would be harmless in comparison with the force of the lower psychology which today is seeking to destroy the power of the human mind.

This is one of the closed doors in human life, and we are trying to open it for the benefit of mankind.

We declare that there is no hell except that which abides in man, or which he makes for himself by his own thought and deeds; no heaven except that which man makes for himself.

❖

The more exalted the dominant motive of the life, the greater is the soul-expression, the more dominant the soul-psychology. The lower the life motive, the stronger becomes the lower self and with it the lower psychology, which so far as it manifests in human life today, is the damnation of humanity.

Nor is this peculiar to our age or to our race, for these dual conflicting forces are as old as humanity itself. How do they manifest? Very simply and in many unsuspected ways. For example, have we not in our experience met with real sermons in poetry, music or art, that lifted us spiritually, above the senses to a higher plane? And, on the other hand, have we not contacted other and evil forces, which played in upon our minds, silently, but nevertheless shutting away the soul-light? We find the play and interplay of the higher and lower psychology on all sides, for as the ancient scripture has it, the *Bhagavad-Gītā:* "These two, light and darkness, are the world's eternal ways."

And then this question of obsession: there are so many theories, so many so-called explanations. But our psychologists have much to learn about it because there exist in the nature invisible and intricate forces which have their connection with the physical brain, and yet can neither be measured nor seen. They exist nevertheless — subtle and powerful forces — that under the pressure of selfish desire will desecrate the loftiest ideals, destroy the highest motives, nullify the best of intentions. They beat in upon the physical brain with play and interplay, and use it to destructive ends.

There is something very wonderful about this brain-mind of ours; there is even something sacred about it because, though it does belong to the physical makeup of man, there still shine upon it as upon a flower the rays of the spiritual sun. But when some selfish desire shuts that light away, there seems no limit to its capacity to be used on lower, destructive lines.

On the other hand, there is no limit to the service the brain-mind can render on the highest spiritual lines, when disciplined and balanced by right education, with the high and immutable principles of a true philosophy of life reflected upon its walls. These are the real mysteries, and they are not studied as they should be.

❖

With all my soul I urge you to *look within*. Even to the man who has lost faith in humanity and in himself, even to the pessimist who dares not think a week ahead in hope — to such as these I say: Look into the chambers of your soul, for truly you are a soul. Rediscover the energy and strength of your manhood. Take time to think, not in the ordinary way, but deeply, and the laws that govern life will be revealed.

You cannot touch the laws connected with this mighty power, the soul-psychology, without generating wonderful forces — forces that the human eye cannot see, that the mind cannot comprehend, cannot explain, but which bring us into touch with nature and with the laws which govern the lower kingdoms of life.

Truly I believe that birds and flowers know us better than we know ourselves; and when we are on the high plane of mystical knowledge, when our hearts are touched with the spiritual forces of nature and of life, we learn to talk with nature, we learn to work with her.

I never went into the woods but the birds sang better while I was there. Not that I gave them the power, but that they, in their simplicity, being part of the great law, felt the longing of my soul for a touch of sweet nature, and they sang to me. I have had some strange experiences in handling flowers; they have answered the yearnings of my soul with just the answer most needed. The tiniest atoms of the earth have voices, and these voices are even a part of ourselves.

And thus in every department of life we can demonstrate the psychology of the soul.

The psychology of the Christos-spirit ever accompanies true manhood and true womanhood. It is the masculine and the feminine blended into the higher unity. Christ had attained that unity — a mystic and interior state — as had other great Teachers before him. And the whole human family can reach this high point of endeavor if it will place itself under the influence of the soul-psychology in life.

Man's only way to win his great hope and to know the truth is to seize hold on himself, assert and realize his potentially all-dominating soul-existence. Making his mind and memory register beyond all future cavil or doubt what he then knows to be true, holding himself at his true dignity, guiding into right conduct all the elements of his nature — his body, mind, and emotions — he will maintain from that moment strength and joy in life. That once done, could he but stand in that attitude for a few weeks or months, he would have made of his mind a willing instrument of service, harnessed it to the chariot of the soul, and dissolved away its limitations.

I am not taking you to a point in space; I am delving down into your heart, trying to bring out what is best in your nature that you may know the higher law. Let there be no delay. There is no need of preparation in the brain-mind sense. You need not memorize catechisms; you have not to spend years in studying your bibles in order to learn the great truths of life and destiny. Your heart will reveal these to you. Once you have found this knowledge and have commenced to apply it to your conduct, you can turn to the Book of the Ages and interpret it in the light of the higher law. You will know your Christ as you never have known him before.

The Path of the Mystic

III

The Light of the Divine

THE mystic is one who lives ever in the consciousness of his divinity. He senses intuitively the divine life in all things. He sees within the outer, which is fleeting and perishable, an inner which is imperishable and eternal.

He in whom the soul is ever active, ever urging to compassionate thought and deed — he is the true mystic.

The path of the mystic is a secret path, in a sense, and a silent and wonderful path. Yet it is open to all men, and is so simple and so near at hand that many who long to tread it yet turn away from it, thinking it to be something else.

If the student will accept the primary truths of theosophy, and will seek to live according to them, every page and every line of *The Secret Doctrine* will have its message for him. But mere book study will avail little; something more than that is required and demanded: the full understanding of the teachings is possible only as the life conforms to those teachings. The true doctrine is secret, hidden; not by the teacher, but in the very nature of the teaching itself, and to gain it, the student must enter by the only door which gives entrance — *the living of the life*.

The one who seeks to fashion his life accordingly will find himself more than an ephemeral spark of Being; he will come to realize that in very truth he is participant in an immortal drama, dating back for millions of years and stretching forward to heights and depths beyond the wildest dreams of poetic imagination. Yet he must learn too that the goal cannot be gained without effort, and that it depends upon himself to take part consciously in the glorious future that awaits the human race, and that conscious cooperation in the uplifting of the race is essential.

Success does not come without effort, without long and often repeated effort, but the intensity and imposed necessity of the struggle, the very desire to make the effort, show that there is already a living power within the heart that demands and will reward beyond all conception strong and unfaltering service. "Progress," said H.P.B., "is made step by step, and each step gained by heroic effort. Conquered passions, like slain tigers, can no longer turn and rend you. Be hopeful, then, not despairing. With each morning's awakening try to live through the day in harmony with the *Higher Self*. 'Try' is the battle-cry, taught by the Teachers to each pupil. Naught else is expected of you. *One who does his best does all that can be asked.*"

❖

The difficulty has been and is, that in making his choice between duty and desire, the disciple has ever two roads before him. He can follow after the vanity of vanities, or seek the mystery of mysteries.

The wrong way is *mis*called the easy way. In reality it is the hard way. The path of self-conquest, if only we travel as we can and as we should — that is the easy way.

There are many ways by which one can follow the easy road, so called, for temptations are everywhere. But he who is willing to follow the road that leads to the light, the road that enables man, conscious of his divinity, to think correctly, to live in the light, and to follow his ideals regardless of the opinions of men — he is one in ten millions.

New opportunities are before us, new demands are being made, for it is a new time. Open the doors of your nature, then, and admit the waiting powers that are outside. The spirit of love is knocking, and opportunities are before you that are undreamed of in their scope.

Once we attune our minds to the great principles of brotherhood and service, our hearts open, our minds clear, and the new light that we long for will break.

If those who sometimes find themselves in a sea of questionings and confusion would just fall back upon the resources of the soul, what strength and peace would come! The soul is a stranger to us, in a sense, and yet it is absolutely resourceful, and when we move out in thought and effort based on pure and high motives, it has always the means at hand to serve us.

A new energy is being liberated from the center of life. This stream of force, for such it is, is felt at first as a mighty Niagara, rushing forward with such rapidity that it threatens to engulf everything; but as it approaches a climax it spreads out in every direction; its currents circulate over the whole earth, and its influence pervades all things. Nothing can rest still; all things are pushed forward by that great solar energy now being set free. Care should be taken that it is not misdirected, and all personal barriers should be removed before they are ground to powder. This force acts everywhere; the gods are its ministrants. There is no need to retire to the woods for the inspiration which it gives, for where the needs of humanity are greatest the presence of the Helpers can be felt most.

We need today a larger faith and trust, and in this we find ourselves living in a condition where everything is possible; where everything we touch will blossom forth and bear gladness and joy to others. Receiving ourselves unstintedly, ungrudgingly, of that large and ample life which animates everything throughout universal space, we shall give freely with open hearts, so that no impoverished life shall ever flow from us.

Many who have reached a certain point sometimes wish to have full explanations given to them so that in some way they may derive personal benefit from the knowledge; but without the stimulus of effort, without

45

trust, without faith, nothing is possible. We go to sleep with full faith that we will arise the next morning. We sow a seed with full faith that nature will perform her part, and the seed spring up and bear fruit.

❖

The great trouble with the human race is that its members do not rightly value the imagination with which they are blessed. It is imagination, recognized as a liberating power, that produces the gems of poetry and art which we so much admire, and it is the mind properly guided by this power which will elevate us all.

I do not believe in miracles, but I hold that the imagination has a wonderful and creative power. I hold that if we let it soar in the world of spiritual and creative thought — and are not afraid to let it soar — it can create what truly seem to be miraculous things.

Yet the imagination, like all things, is dual. Along lower lines it is as disintegrative in its power as it is creative and constructive on higher lines.

Visualize! Visualize! You touch a mystic law when you create in imagination the picture of mighty things, for you open a door to new powers within yourself. Something in the way of potent energies is awakened and called into life and strength both without you and within. If you aspire, visualize your aspirations. Make a mind-picture of your spiritual ideals, a picture of the spiritual life as you know it to be, and carry that picture with you day by day. Cherish it as a companion. Carry it with you for breakfast, dinner and supper, and before you know it a new life has been born. Before you know it the ideal has become the real and you have taken your place as a creator, truly, in the great, divine scheme of life.

The Open Doors of Silence

The power of silence! It is in the silence that we shall find the key, if we choose to search for it, that will open books of revelation in our natures. We shall find there a strength that has never been ours before and that never could be until we sought this path. We shall find there the peace that passeth understanding. It may not come in a moment, nor in accord with puny wishes and desires, but if the motive is unselfish, *it will come.*

It steals into the life, into the heart and mind, like the grandest symphonies in music. It carries you above and out of and beyond your difficulties and your trials, and prepares you for the real life. The silence! The one touch of silent prayer!

When a man in the silence becomes conscious of his own divine nature, he realizes if only for a moment that he is different from what he seems. He begins to feel that he is a god; he begins to let the imagination pulse through his heart, telling him of mighty things beyond ordinary comprehension, to feel something of his duty to humanity. This is discipline.

Discipline comes in many ways, but theosophy shows one how a man, without help of book or creature, may yet find his own inner power, be no longer a mere potentiality. He will dig into the depths of his being that he may find wisdom. He will discover within himself a new quality of intuition and, at last, when touched by the 'feel' of this diviner life, the power of self-discipline will come to him, and he can stand and say: *I know!*

The more we are united in the silence in the attempt at self-purification, the nearer we are to the light.

Never can we lose sight of the light, never of our obligations or our divinity, if we are to realize the sacredness of our calling. There is so much in these few words: the sacredness of one's calling!

There is something growing in our hearts and in our daily lives that cannot be described, that can only be felt. But once felt, deeply, profoundly, we are then moving along the true path. We are rarefying the air; we are sanctifying life.

❖

Let us not forget that we are working together for the purpose of serving humanity and bringing to it the knowledge that it needs; that this is not a commercial effort, nor simply an ordinary educational effort, *but that it is a spiritual effort in the highest sense;* and for that reason we must be spiritually endowed with those qualities that make for true nobility.

I echo the words of my predecessor, William Quan Judge: "There is no idleness for the Mystic. He finds his daily life among the roughest and hardest of the labors and trials of the world perhaps, but goes his way with smiling face and joyful heart, nor grows too sensitive for association with his fellows, nor so ex-

49

tremely spiritual as to forget that some other body is perhaps hungering for food."

For we are one in essence; there *is* the interblending of forces so delicate, so subtle, that they cannot be perceived on this plane, yet they are ever at work, making or marring the destiny of a soul.

There is self-destruction, even on physical lines, in carrying an atmosphere of wrong thought. We have it in our power not only to build our bodies into health, but to retain that health very much longer than the allotted threescore years and ten. I hold it a duty to work towards this end, by right thinking and abstemious and thoughtful living. Moreover, in such an effort, if it is made unselfishly, we can positively temper our bodies, much as metal can be tempered, so that they are unaffected by things that would put a strain upon them ordinarily.

You must take time for self-analysis. There must be time for the calm, reflective attitude of mind. Study the conditions surrounding you, the motives that actuate you in this or that effort or work, and determine with absolute honesty whether they are selfish, unselfish, or mixed. This will be an uplifting, a clarifying process, for the conscience is at work. It is a confession, really, to the higher self, the divinity within you.

You invoke in such an effort the magic power latent in the silences of life. False ideas are gradually eliminated under such a process, and true ones find their way in. Things once deemed necessary to the personal life become no longer so; and in thus moving out into a larger field of thought and aspiration you move towards self-adjustment.

In such thought you eliminate your weaknesses, and you learn also one great truth, a truth accentuated by the Nazarene: that you cannot serve two masters. You cannot move in opposite directions at one and the same time; you cannot ride two horses at once; and those who try it are certain to find themselves, sooner or later, arriving nowhere and more than likely trampled under the feet of both.

Think on these things in the silence; and remember that when a selfish or personal thought creeps in during silence, the door is shut and the light cannot find its place; the soul is barred, and the day will bring little to you that will satisfy the better side of your nature.

51

In the true condition of mind and heart there arises a sweet peace, which does not descend upon us from above, for we are in the midst of it. It is not like the sunshine, for no transitory clouds obscure its rays, but it is permanent and ever-abiding through all the days and years. Nothing can move us when this condition is reached.

We have but to take the first step in the true spirit of brotherliness, and all other steps will follow in natural sequence. We have to be warriors and fight the old fight unceasingly, but leagued with us in this ancient fight are all the hosts of light. Behind man, back of all things, broods the eternal spirit of compassion.

❖

Humanity has long wandered through the dark valley of bitter experiences; but the mountain heights are again seen, suffused with the glow of dawn and the promise of a new Golden Age; a pathway is once more shown to that realm where the gods abide.

See the gates of life and peace standing open before you, if you have but faith and trust to enter in. But none can enter alone; each must bring with him the sad and sorrowing. None can cross the threshold alone, but must help to bear the burdens of the over-burdened, must aid the feeble steps of those who are discouraged, must support those who are bowed down with sin and despair; and as he sends out the radiation of that joy and strength which he receives from his own aspirations and devotion to the higher self, joy and strength and power shall enter into the lives of these others, and together they shall pass through into Life.

A vow is an action rising like a star high above the level of the common deeds of life. It is a witness that the outer man has at that moment realized its union with the inner, and the purpose of its existence, registering a great resolve to become one with the Father in Heaven.

At that moment the radiant path of light is seen with the eye of pure vision, the disciple is reborn, the old life is left behind, he enters a new way. For a moment he feels the touch of a guiding hand ever stretched out to him from the inner chamber. For a moment his ear catches the harmonies of the soul.

53

All this and more is the experience of those who make this vow with their whole hearts, and as they constantly renew it, and constantly renew their endeavor, the harmonies come again and again, and the clear path is once more beheld.

They carry the inspiration into outer life, and energize with it their common duties, high and low: gain from it strength for self-sacrifice, and thus bringing the inner into the outer, pouring forth in deeds that wine of divine life of which they have learned to partake, they achieve, little by little, the harmony of perfect life. Each effort carves the path of the next, and in no long time one single moment's silence will bring forth to the disciple's aid the strength of his soul.

Nature, the Mystic Mother

Think of nature in her splendor and her glory, her supreme, divine willingness to serve, of how she stands in the silence, urging us to the better things of life! Then think of music — of how it steals into our souls and our lives, bringing us, if only for a moment, into a unity and concord of spirit such as are rarely found. Could we hold the feeling born of such experiences, could we carry their inspiration with us from morning to night, from night to morning, in our duties, our struggles, our sorrows, our battles in the great arena of life — joy would indeed abide with us, even with suffering as our lot.

Nature is so beneficent, so ready to heal and bless. When the pressure of cares and trials is almost too great to be borne and I feel the need of help in finding a larger patience, I go to nature, and there I find it again and again. She is the mystic mother of us all.

You cannot observe nature without realizing that there is within and behind the outer an *inner*, a center of mystic life. In her more beautiful aspects she has attained to something which humanity lacks. And yet when the human touch is given there is a response: the flower that is nurtured by man's hand becomes a more beautiful flower, because there is a spiritual unity in the efforts of man and nature, working together. One whose heart is touched with the love of these things is growing spiritually and someday will find the great, the profounder, meaning of life.

Every time the wind blows it is singing you a song of the gods. Every time a flower blossoms it is bringing you a message from the higher law. Every time you hear the ocean as it beats against the shore and recedes in musical rhythm, it is speaking to your soul — a voice from nature, verily a voice from God. The magnitude, the grandeur of these things, the possibilities folded within them — these can truly be sensed only in the silence.

But alas! we do not pause; we will not listen to the inner voice that is ever calling us to the better things of life. We have no time — or so we think; we are in the whirl and nightmare of delusion. The glory of the higher law is little perceived by the multitude; the grandeur of nature is not felt as it might be, nor is music, nor the diviner silent harmonies of our own higher selves. We are hidebound in our prejudices and misconceptions, and — let me say it plainly — in our ignorance. So that in spite of the royal, divine light within us, we are in the shadows and we cannot find our way.

When I look out over the world and see humanity with its unbrotherliness and despair, if it were not for the birds and flowers, the trees and the blue overhead,

I could not bear the picture: I should lose heart. But between mankind and nature a mystic alliance exists, and this, once recognized and acknowledged, becomes a redemptive power.

Every day has its brightness, its bloom, its color; every day is the happiest I ever lived. There is no thought of yesterday or tomorrow, only the joy of living today, the happiness of the passing moment, the unity of all life and the noble plan of life universal. I see on one side forces of darkness, on the other those of light; but I do not dwell on the dark side. I turn my eyes to greet the rising sun.

A new hope is dawning on humanity. This hope is the mainspring of progression and the evidence of it can be seen everywhere; the great heart of nature pulsates with joy, as it did in the days preceding the dawn of the dark age. Men and women who have so long borne the heavy burden of life, whose hearts have been well-nigh broken by the weight of many sorrows, feel the new joy awakened by the great symphonies of harmony which are now being sounded. It is felt in the heart of man and gives rise to constant aspiration; it is the quality which makes him great.

57

The golden light is shining; the herald of the morning proclaims the message of love anew; the ripples of the waves on the seashore lisp the glad song; the breeze bears it on its bosom; the tints of the flowers convey it; it shines forth from the stars in their sparkling brilliance; the great blue dome above suggests it; the birds warble it forth from every tree; the newborn babe is a complete revelation of it; the eyes of the loved ones passing into the great beyond impart the strength and courage of that great hope, and point to a future day when they shall return again to carry on their work. For hope incarnates from age to age, and where hope dwells, beauty and love abide for ever.

The Law is immutable and Love is eternal.

Yet, as in every advance that nature makes, as the cycles in their wheeling course come round, there are some who lag behind and lose sight of their heritage, blinded by the desire for personal gain, by ambition and love of power; so that today there are some who refuse the opportunity that for ages their souls have waited for. The cycles have brought them and ourselves to the point of former achievement and former failure. We and they have met in the past as in this life, and shall meet again in the future, and by our action today we are forging the links that shall help or mar their progress, as well as our own and that of all humanity, in the future.

But the crucial point of the cycle is past; the fiercest ordeal is over; no powers in heaven or hell can longer stay the onward progress of humanity. The hosts of light are already victorious.

Teacher and Student

IV

The Beaming Thought

A PURE, strong, unselfish thought, beaming in the mind, lifts the whole being to the heights of light. From this point can be discerned, to a degree, the sacredness of the moment and the day.

When the disciple begins consciously to deepen and broaden his life according to the highest law of his being, he must remember that confusion of ideas, behind which lies desire, will meet him at every step. The beaming thought as the Watcher and Master, recognized as such, becomes the helping power.

Dismiss the things of the world, its ways, its interests and its limited habits of thought. Kill out in yourselves the desire for these and find the larger life. Truly, these selfish desires and demands are but phantoms placed in your way by karma, called up by karma out of the past of yourselves and revivified with a false and seeming life by the very force of your aspirations.

Why not recognize them as such, see them for what they are, dismiss them once and for all, and look through the mists of self and desire to the sublime reality beyond?

The very fact that you find stumbling blocks in your way should give you an influx of courage, a positive joy, because of the opportunity thus presented to you to cast them away forever. Self-conquest! Is that not what you are here for? Is it not what your soul led you here for? Is it not one of the very things that attracted you to theosophy — a great objective, an ideal, a mystic goal? Why not, then, look at the matter squarely and act without fear or compromise? Every time you compromise on this vital point, remember, you are holding back the world's great reconstructive work and just so many more hungry souls are left starving for the bread of the spirit. Move away from limitations and delusions and step into the larger life!

❖

The cry of the present day is for receipts — receipts for this or that, brain-mind directions for everything, from how to succeed in business to how to talk with Mars. The soul does not need receipts. Study these words from the writings of William Quan Judge, reflecting truths as old as the universe itself:

"Those who ask for particularity of advice are not yet grown to the stature of a hero who, being all, dareth all; who, having fought many a fight in other lives, rejoices in his strength and fears neither life nor death, neither sorrow nor abuse, and wishes no ease himself while others suffer."

If you are in the right place, at the right time, and working in the right way, you have nothing in the universe to fear. If you are following your duty with that discrimination and resourcefulness that belongs to you as a soul, you *are* in the right place and working in the best possible way, however humble the duty may seem to be. "Nothing is great, nothing is small in the divine economy."

It is necessary, however, to discriminate between what is your duty and what is not; and the brain-mind cannot help you here. More than likely it will simply be in your way. You will have to seek refuge in the intuitional part of your nature, for intuition is the real, the mystic teacher. It is the voice of the soul in man.

65

A teacher may endeavor to impart the truth, but if the intuition of the pupil is not developed, at least to a degree, the effort is useless. We have not the intuition of the ancients.

We cannot bring great ideals into concrete expression until *we* are the living expression of those ideals. We cannot set right the affairs of the world in a way that shall build spiritually for the future, until our lives are based absolutely right. The nations are wandering today, and their statesmen admit as much, but no one can help them in a lasting way whose own little nation — *the individual life* — is not spiritually what it should be.

We cannot afford to be negative, for the opposing forces are active, and if we allow the moments to be unguarded, or neglect to fill the time with creative images and invigorating thoughts, these moments will be seized by the "enemy" and become surcharged with inimical energies and agencies.

Disintegrative forces are especially active and dangerous at the present time, owing to the general unrest, and are apt to work upon us destructively when we are asleep. That is, if we are will-less or negative. So that we should take the last half-hour before retiring, for spiritual rest, constructive thought, quiet, silent reflection on spiritual things. Such a course would place us beyond the reach of disintegrative agencies during those hours when the soul is free.

We are not so much at their mercy when awake, in a sense, for then we are on guard instinctively. But in sleep the body is in certain ways unprotected, *unless* guarded by the silent warrior-force of our aspirations and spiritual will.

In sleep the soul is free, winging its way into new spaces, finer worlds of thought and feeling, evolving, growing, expanding — and it longs to carry you with it, the *you* of prosaic daily life. The soul is within you — and yet it is not: there is a mystery here.

Harmony is the key to all occult advance, and it is a knowledge of its laws and the relations of sound, number and color as applied and directed by the pupils that enables the teacher to strike the higher tones and awake the spiritual vision. The forces have gone to the ends of the world, and opportunities for labor and success will be had such as none have dreamed of.

67

Your Spiritual Strength

Kill out timidity! Kill out fear! We are constantly upon the fringe of great opportunities and at some crucial point; and then, instead of grasping these opportunities and moving on to a larger view and a broader spiritual life, we shrink, we hold back through timidity — and so we lose them all. The present is an unusual cycle, and never in this life will we meet present opportunities again.

Let us be careful, in making this forward step, that we do not ungird our armor through fear.

Fear nothing, for every renewed effort raises all former failures into lessons, all sins into experiences. Understand me when I say that in the light of renewed effort the karma of all your past alters; it no longer threatens. It passes from the plane of penalty before the soul's eye, up to that of tuition. It stands as a monument, a reminder of past weakness, and a warning against future failure.

So fear nothing for yourself; you are behind the shield of your reborn endeavor, though you have failed a hundred times. Try slowly to make it your motive for fidelity that others may be faithful. Fear only to fail in your duty to others, and even then let your fear be for *them*, not yourself. Not for thousands of years have the opposing forces been so accentuated. Not one of you can remain neutral; if you think you can, and seek to do so, in reality you are adding your powers to those of darkness and lending your strength to the forces of evil. The cry has gone out to each, and each must choose. This is your opportunity.

Will you have it recorded that your vow was of the lips or of the heart? You have studied and thought, many of you long and faithfully; bring forth the fruit of this now as action, for the hour has struck. Humanity calls for aid. Who of you has the strength, the will to go forward?

We live very little *in* our bodies, actually *in* them; we live rather in a world of ideas and aspirations above and about us. Our great task is to bring these ideas and aspirations into concrete expression, to make them actual, practical; in a word, to make them into *deeds*. And in doing this we must learn to follow lines of least resistance, ever trusting in the Law.

To gain freedom, you will have to accentuate the spirit of brotherly love; to gain it you will have to work for it, also, and work understandingly. And yet it is so easy, so simple. If you hold close to duty, and keep a sweet, impersonal love burning in your heart, all the rest will come; and that has its practical application in many ways. For example, if you do not like another, if you do not like to work with him when it is a duty to do so, consider that a challenge, and stand up and meet the test. That is practical brotherhood.

There is nothing so lamentable as to see one who has touched our philosophy go on with duty half-heartedly. He is robbing the future and his own life of something that his soul is actually crying for. If you avoid issues which come up now in your lives, you will have to meet them later on and probably with less help than you have now.

Let it be remembered that the teacher's work, the real work, *has naught to do with words written or spoken.* In the past, when vibratory forces were still understood, words were never used or looked for in the conveyance of the higher teachings. Let me make this clearer:

Listen to the note of a bell resounding; its vibrations get fainter and fainter, but though there comes at last a point, different for different people, when the sound is utterly lost for the outer ear, we know that the thrill is broadening out, and will forever go on doing so, into eternal and boundless space. And especially where the note is from a human voice it carries out with it *a quality from the consciousness* of him who sent it forth.

The presence of the soul is eternally manifest — to the degree that you hold to the path of right action, to the degree that you love and aspire and strive. You must cultivate a larger trust, a larger hope. And there must be constant, quiet effort on a thoroughly balanced line, without this spasmodic shifting up and down. Holding to calmness and balance, striving continually and with no concern as to results, before you know it the victory will be yours.

Your spiritual energy grows day by day and hour by hour just so far as you permit it to grow and help it to evolve. It is a force that is very real and immensely powerful — a potent force that becomes, if you do not prevent it, a great wheel of activity in the universe.

71

People copy each other too much; it is a universal human tendency. But you should not do so; aside from the fact that you are all so very unlike, having evolved differently and through different experiences, you have immense resources spiritually if you but draw upon them. Each of you should learn to build your own atmosphere. Strike out on your own lines, not another's. In brief, have the courage to *be yourselves.*

Dare to be yourself — your greater self! Dare to leap forward and be something you never before knew it was in you to be! Dare to move out and upward in the strength of your soul and find something new in your makeup. It is a critical time for everyone who aspires, for many things are in the balance. The need is for energy, aspiration, trust, and the power of the spiritual will. "The more one dares, the more he shall obtain."

❖

Think of the effort we have made to vitalize our theosophical work by protesting against the cold intellectualism of the age. The influence of this has spread out and has reached the so-called leaders of the time. In spite of the selfishness of the age, the heart-doctrine is permeating all strata of society. Yet how much, how very, very much, remains to be done.

One who declares himself a student of theosophy, in that moment invokes his higher nature, the warrior-quality of his soul. He also invokes the divine law which governs his life. He makes a larger demand upon that law and declares himself to be more receptive to it.

As to vigilance: how attentive we are to the material part of our lives in the sense of being vigilant! How much more attentive, as humanity goes, than to the spiritual! But as students of theosophy we have a sacred duty: to study the duality of our nature and take a stand for vigilance in the inner life. Let us see that the help which goes out from us to another is help to the higher self. Vigilance on our part will give us power to render such help. Vigilance in spiritual things – that is the supreme need.

The loyal and truehearted are always on the alert; they are ever ready. For them the gods are not a procession of phantoms, but living realities. They know how to profit by each new opportunity, and each day sees them at their post, ready for their allotted work.

73

For them the granite and clay are luminous creations, resplendent with color, rich with enchantment. Unclouded by doubt or suspicion, they falter not nor fail.

Do not worry; do not fear; do not think about results. Set plans come from the brain-mind, and in creative work this cannot be allowed to rule. There is a method of fashioning the life so that this will not be; then the brain-mind will keep its place as the servant, not the tormentor of the soul. It is something to think about when you get up in the morning and when you retire at night. It is very close to what I mean when I speak of trust in the higher law.

As writers you are so often carried away with your themes and with the fear that you will not do them justice. If you could only learn the meaning of preparation — *preparation* in the theosophic sense. If you would only take part of the time at your command, however limited, for *spiritual preparation*, never taking up your pen until you are mentally *in order,* a book of revelations would come.

Effecting difficult things while they are easy, and managing great things in their beginnings — this is the way, as the sages of antiquity have taught. The wise man takes account of small things and so never has any difficulty. "Transact your business before it takes form."

Practice accuracy in every detail of thought, speech and action. While you need not look for results, results will speak to you and bring encouragement. Practice punctuality in everything. Promptness and neatness mean economy of time, money, material, energy and thought.

Practice system. This means a methodical arrangement of time, work and material, and also a methodical arrangement of thinking. Remember that system is a channel for effective utilization of one's forces.

In offering suggestions to others, remember that every suggestion carries in it a measure of criticism. Let your criticism *begin at home*. As H. P. Blavatsky says: "Be more severe with yourself than with others; be more charitable towards others than towards yourself."

There is always the superb energy of eternity in the heart of one who does his best. If at the moment when this is felt the man would pause, reflect and meditate, he would find his way to the light. The mysteries of his nature, of his own inner self, would be revealed to him.

❖

As we move out into the future with this mighty soul-urge of universal love, we implant in the very atmosphere in which we live and breathe a something that was not there before — seeds that take root and grow and blossom in the hearts of all with whom we come in contact. So that, since these things are true, there must be a forgetfulness of self, a confidence superb in its power, a soul-confidence that will impregnate our very mental atmosphere with a wisdom that can be breathed in mentally by all those we meet.

And I hold that just so far as an individual makes his life true, strong, powerful, and selfless, just so far is he building mighty and glorious ideals for the future — ideals that the world cannot today comprehend, but that are recorded upon the mystic screen of time, although they may stand waiting for ages for our minds to understand them fully and for our souls to live up to them.

Unbrotherliness is the insanity of the age, as I have often said; and those who cultivate the feeling of separateness and self give evidence at times of the very absence of the ego. Truly the soul is not there. Unkindly criticism heaps up a terrible karma, for it shuts the soul away.

❖

Climb! Ever keep climbing! The path winds upward — this wonderful path of self-mastery — but to the unselfish and courageous it is a path of victory and joy. Throw away the lower viewpoint, right out of your lives! You must unite for self-conquest; then all other things will come.

Difficult as it must be for you to believe what I say, yet it is true that the Kingdom of Heaven is nearer at hand than you can realize, and that all the storms, trials and sorrows that we see now raging in human life are but indications of the passing away of the old order of things. All that we have to do is to seize our opportunities, do faithfully our duties as they lie before us, ingrain in the very atmosphere in which we live the finer vibrations of the higher law, study and work, work and study.

Let us no longer crucify the Christ in ourselves. Bid him come forth and enter upon his noble work

77

now, for the woes of humanity are great. See you not that this is the crucial moment for you to grasp the hand of your Warrior-companion reached out to you, to lead you on and up to the realm where your thoughts and deeds will be those of gods? Stand unfailingly on guard, the sentinel of your own inner chamber, vigilant against the entry there of the least of the lurking foes about the doorway of the sanctum. Through that doorway goes and returns the soul, and it is your task to see that it is unimpeded in its freedom to act and to help.

The Helpers of the race, the Elder Brothers, have trod, as we now tread, the dark valley to win final liberation. Our path is easier because they have already traversed it, easier yet because of the love and compassion they send back to us.

Oh, that every atom in my being were a thousand-pointed star to help men see the divine everywhere, to know their limitless power, to feel while in the body the exhaustless joy of real life, to wake and live instead of dreaming the heavy dreams of this living death, to know themselves as at once part of and directors of universal law. This is our birthright of wisdom, and the hour of attainment is *now* if we will.

A teacher is one who leads you to the light; who shows you how to summon to your aid the help that lies hidden in the silences of life, in the silences of time and space, in the low, silent chambers of duty. But you must do your part.

There is a state of consciousness that is an open way to the light. Karma is lifting the veil, and we can, if we will, look to the future with that certainty that is born only of pure motive. We are indeed at the pivotal point of our world's history, and are called upon to act our part nobly, wisely, courageously, dispassionately, and justly.

Teacher and student are links in a great spiritual chain, extending from infinity to infinity, from past to future. Invisible and intangible, this nevertheless exists, a golden chain of spiritual life, a great reality. As a link in this chain, man becomes both giver and receiver, passing on the torch of truth from hand to hand, from nation to nation, and from age to age.

The Heart-cry of the World

V

The Vortex of Human Life

THE world is crying out for help, for hope. But this can never come save from those who know their own natures, who cannot be deceived by the subtle voice of evil, whose lives show forth the guiding presence of the soul in every act and thought, who shed at every moment the blood of their compassion. The heart-cry of the world is a prayer to the higher law, a longing for better things.

Seeing the misery of the world as I do, and coming in close contact in correspondence with hundreds of despairing souls, I feel the urging of that great heart of humanity to plead with you to make a new effort, and to seek every moment of the day to strengthen that effort by noble deeds and by pure thoughts and actions. If each would do his part in this, all the rest would care for itself.

The great whirling vortex of human life holds the mind in a nightmare of delusion. Humanity is stifled and the world held down and back by the psychology of pessimism. So many have no faith in themselves, no faith in each other. Some are pleading for help and light, it is true, for something that can still the craving of the heart, but so many are content with the superficial. And this black psychology, sweeping in, affects to some degree the minds of all. Even the strongest, the best, find it a constant struggle to live up to their possibilities because of this subtle, disintegrative force. Yet to everyone who seriously pushes forward in spite of this, a new door opens with each day, a new cycle — truly, a new world.

The whole mass of humanity is a psychological field on inner planes, a vast aggregation of opposing forces, some pushing towards light and harmony, but the great bulk of them against advancement and against the truth.

The great onward rush of human effort for better things is intense, very intense, yet so many wander away from the path of light. Losing sight of their divinity, the godlike, guiding power within, they wander this way and that, searching this way and that, through this book and that, and so on, all along the way. Their faces, their words, their writings, tell the story of disillusionment and failure. And the remedy? Does it not lie in the finding of the SELF?

The present is a critical time, and if we are to reach that point at which peace of mind is possible, we must accentuate the divinity of man — and so beautifully, so truly, that the questions of injustice which now cannot be answered will then be explained.

Under the pressure of all that is happening in the world — much that is seen now and *much that will be seen later* in the spirit of unbrotherliness, running into insanity and despotism — our vow becomes a beacon-light in our hearts, a beacon-light in the world. Let us bathe in the spirit of it, illumine our minds by the light of it. Let us fortify ourselves, and protest, not only against the evil in our own natures but against evil said of another, and the evildoing of those who take the name of truth to cloak their unrighteousness.

It matters not how much money we may accumulate, how much scholastic learning we may possess, how many magnificent structures we may erect in the name of civilization. Unless we arrive at a better understanding of brotherly toleration, we are working in vain for the future.

In our selfish indifference as a people we are unconsciously taking part in the crimes of the world; we are absolutely factors in these crimes. Only because we have lost the power of spiritual discrimination are we able to view the present conditions with equanimity. We have been taught to judge by appearances, to perceive the physical, outer man and the brain-mind alone; we have ignored the existence of the inner life, the real self of man, that which looks behind the veils of illusion and sees things as they are. We are arrant cowards if we do not begin to think and work and hope along new lines, when the whole world is crying out for help.

To reach the truth there must be in the aspiring mind a certain quality of resolution, determination; and yet the truth is all about us, sweeping as on invisible currents into the very atmosphere in which we live. It is as though brooding over the world in its sorrow were a great urge, a great soulful power, standing between Deity and man's endeavor to rise and go unto his own. It is the real intermediator, and one feels its presence when in one's highest mood. One cannot think of the battlefields across the water, the devastated nations, the deserted homes, the neglected, persecuted children, without feeling something of its power. And the question arises: shall mankind go backward, hardened, cynical, skeptical and discouraged, or push forward and upward with these new currents of life?

❖

If we fail to understand ourselves, if we fail in our duty to the higher self, we are absolutely out of place in attempting to help others. For how can we help our brothers understandingly unless we understand ourselves? We shall overdo or underdo or perhaps not do anything at all.

Only a few, a very few, are willing to take trouble for humanity, and as long as this is the case we may expect menacing conditions in our civilization. Many people with splendid possibilities seem to be so near — almost touching, in fact — the fringe of the great truth. But they close their eyes to the need, they turn away and walk on, satisfied with their own little path because to do otherwise is "too much trouble." Nevertheless, because of the thought and effort of just the few who love humanity, a benediction is certain to come. In time our thought-life will become rarefied;

men's minds will be touched with a new power sprung from the optimism and the hope of the few who defend the truth. We shall look down over the hills and into the valleys and see godlike men and women walking there; we shall feel ere long the influence, the mighty overshadowing, of a new civilization.

In the heart-touch is the saving quality which will redeem humanity and bring about universal brotherhood. The word charity should be eliminated. In the name of charity men and women have been treated like so much personal baggage and labeled accordingly. Out of the great heart of nature all things proceed, and all things lead back there at last; all worlds and systems of worlds, from the great central sun to the smallest particle in space, must thrill responsive to the pulsations of that infinite heart of compassion. The Great Mother reaches forth to receive her own. All efforts to retard are less than insignificant. In every act which partakes of the divine quality of infinite compassion lies concealed the potency of all the spheres. All nature obeys the command of one whose heart beats constantly for others.

Infinite patience and infinite love are required in dealing with the weaknesses of humanity. Oh, that love could flow freely through the hearts of all men, uncolored by personality. Then a new day would dawn, verily.

The Day of Achievement is Here

The hero of today must be a hero of heroes. The ideal must no longer be left remote from life, but made divinely human, close and intimate, as of old. *Now* is the day of resurrection. Man looking up will see the old ideals restored, and seeing, live.

My hopes go out in the very atoms of the air. They are sounded in the silences of the night, when the world is sleeping and the veil is lifted for a space between the weaknesses of those who suffer and their aspirations.

In our love for poor humanity, let us salute the Law in a warriorlike spirit; and let us call forth from our hearts a new inspiration, breathing itself into a new tone of silent, calm effort for peace and light everywhere. Let it be a radiation of the diviner life within

89

ourselves, binding us to the "new order of ages" that we have chosen to build.

Great as have been the discoveries of the past century, still greater are those to follow. Greater exponents of art will be born among us; they will present higher standards and create grander ideals. Literature will gain a new impetus from the new creators who will come to serve the masses with a "feast of reason and a flow of soul" on lines never dreamed of in modern times. Science will astonish the age with its discoveries of some of nature's finer forces.

But the greatest development is not to be looked for on the material plane and in physical science and invention; more marvelous still will be the unfolding of the nature of man on spiritual and mental lines. The possibilities that lie before us in these directions would, if presented today, meet only with incredulity and condemnation, for in this material age man cannot understand the heights that may be attained through self-mastery.

❖

We should not become so absorbed in the little achievement of today as to render it impossible for us to receive the key to the wider knowledge of the future. If we could realize the voice of the soul working behind the ordinary mentality, we should consciously become receptive to higher influences and more spiritual realities; we should bring about that condition within ourselves where we should hear the divine melodies, restoring harmony throughout all nature. In this way we should become pioneers, opening up the vision of men to the vast and unexplored regions of life, and being conscious of this possibility, so stimulate every energy that the very atoms in space, the atoms composing every organism, would change and begin to respond to the divine impulse.

Man was born into this world to attain, and to do this he must struggle as the child struggles to pass through the gates of birth. To attain he must surmount conditions, break through all limitations, and persevere in effort until he reaches spiritual perfection. If we only had the courage to step out into the realm of real thought – for that realm holds the great secrets of human nature which are the real mysteries of life.

Progressive as we are in many ways, we have not yet touched the key to that remedial power that alone

91

can lift the burdens from the people. Something more than material wealth is needed, something more than intellectual accumulation. For intellectualism has no lasting power without the practice of the highest morality.

The first step to be taken in occultism is the practice of unselfishness, for all work for humanity should be performed without thought of reward. Such work is of greater importance than the mere cultivation of the intellect or the collection of large libraries.

Foreshadowings

[Excerpts from editorials appearing in 1897 and 1898.]

Are there not, in our civilization today, signs that mark a unique barbarism among us, showing an immense danger of retrogression? Can we not see, in spite of all the good there is in the world, that the very blood of some of our brothers is teeming with a heartless cruelty, a subtle viciousness, and a monstrous selfishness and hypocrisy? Is not the world brimful of unrest, unhappiness, injustice and despair; and are we not on the very edge of a condition which, if not improved, must sweep away the bright prospects of our present civilization?

Today, as a people, we are by our thoughts and actions affecting to no small degree the record of the next century. We are adding one more link to the chain of events on both the lower and the higher planes of evolution. It is high time that we eliminate from our minds unfaith and egotism, cynicism and selfishness, and prepare ourselves to be a part of the great movement of spiritual life which is now close at hand.

The world seems mad today, moving towards a point at the end of this cycle where only staunch, firm, tempered hearts can turn this tide in the affairs of men to a higher plane of action.

Viewing the present striking aspects, can we for one moment be satisfied to live contentedly and selfishly in the shadow of darkness and unrest? Is it possible for anyone having one grain of human pity in the heart, or love of truth and justice, to do aught but work, work all the time unflinchingly and unselfishly, for his brother man and all creatures — not apart from but among them, with a courage that obscures all thought of self?

We should regard present events as transitory, leading to a more permanent and higher development. Indeed, we should learn practical wisdom through these varied and trying experiences. We must stand face to face with facts in the life of the world.

We can find light shining in dark places if we do not externally hold to forms and appearances. If we can but exert ourselves to think above the atmosphere of doubt and despair, we can find peace even amid the whirl and restlessness of life.

Now is the time, for at the end of this century [19th] an opportunity is given to humanity that it has not had for thousands of years. The cycle has reached its point of swiftest momentum; an effort made today has greater effect than at any other point of the cycle. It is like the ninth wave on the seashore which the fisherman waits for, that he may bring his smack safely to land. Today a small effort brings great results; today sudden progress can be made that could not be accomplished before in months or even years. Today is the great opportunity to enter the Path.

But this cannot be accomplished unless men realize the essential divinity of their own natures. True progress begins with this step alone. Too long has poor humanity been living on the outer edge of truth and light; too long has help been sought from without; too long has the inner divine nature been obscured and the shadows of external life mistaken for the reality.

Unconsciously we may be playing into the hands of the Brothers of the Shadow by a careless thought, a lightly spoken word. We may thus strengthen their destructive work until what was in us a thought, becomes a terrific force, gathering momentum as it goes, until finally it results in some national calamity.

We cannot be too careful, let it be reiterated. The destiny of the nation lies in the hands of the people; today we stand on the verge of great changes. Let us realize, then, our individual responsibility, and let us by steadfast integrity uphold the true principles of brotherhood.

❖

At the close of the year 1897, amidst the turmoil and unrest engendered by the titanic forces of good

and evil contending for the mastery of the coming
centuries, are heard the silvery notes of the Christmas
bells and the loving voice of the Christos — bidding
men cease their selfish strife and their mad race for
power and gain, calling them to turn their faces to the
light and unite their hearts and voices in one great
anthem of brotherly love, of peace and goodwill to all
creatures; and urging us with courage and patience
to brace our inner natures against all that seeks to
lead us from the true path, that we may gain greater
strength to do our whole duty to our fellowmen.

The Cry of the Nations for Peace

It is a great reflection upon the mind of a nation
that there should be war instead of peace, brute force
instead of the forces of mind and soul. For human
thought is measureless in its power, and the spiritual
will could bring about universal peace and absolutely
maintain it, would man but evoke it.

The nations are praying for peace; but lasting
peace can never be attained until the spirit of true
brotherhood is manifested in the hearts of men.

We could not expect universal peace at once; I know too much of human nature for that. We must learn to trust each other first, individuals and nations both, and we must broaden our ideas as to the meaning of brotherhood. In all the nations today we find great minds bent upon this problem, sincere men and women who are profoundly interested in the welfare of the world. But oh, the time that is wasted, the brain oil used, the faculties energized to bring about a new order of things in the name of peace — while they have lost sight of the true, the simple, the only way to do it.

Brotherhood is the way; that is the keynote of the new age. *Universal brotherhood means universal peace.*

Men may talk of peace, and work for peace, but it is mockery unless they try to find peace within their own natures. You cannot gain the power to adjust civic affairs, let alone international affairs, until you begin self-adjustment.

"But," some judicial mind may say, "how can we hold the nations of the world at peace when differences exist, seemingly irreconcilable differences?" My reply must be: what holds together a family when

97

differences arise? Kinship, the basic love of brother for brother that is teeming within its life. That will suffice to hold it together always if it has grown and evolved in the spirit of justice. Why not, then, the larger family of the world?

Why is not humanity aroused to its great need *before* disasters come? Why cannot we help each other *before* we are challenged by suffering or by war? Why cannot we move out beyond our limitations, in true compassion and with true love of justice, and ingrain into human life the spirit of brotherhood? Spiritual growth — that is the ideal. It is the only guarantee of permanent peace.

Yet, in spite of enormous limitations, a larger work for humanity is being done, the real work is truly going on. But it is being accomplished largely in the silences of life. I believe that the great divine voice of humanity in its nobler aspect is even now trying to reach us, trying to attract our vision to the grander life, to broader horizons, to more infinite vistas, that we may dream, if only for an hour, of better things.

Let us give way to the eternal processional of the peace-bringers, the currents of divinity ever ready to

98

flow through every man who will take down the bars and evoke their passage. We are fixed; they change ever. We are mechanical; they are spontaneous. Fatigue is ours; they are immortal, ever-born and never-fading.

Let us, by playing our part well, evoke the god of peace, that it may brood over our world and breathe into the hearts of all a larger tolerance and a greater love for each other, for all nations and all people.

A living wedge is cleaving the darkness of the darkest age. We are witnesses to that compassion which is the light itself. The hour of right action is here.

The crest-wave of spiritual effort! A sublime and unselfish purpose will carry us to that high point — and then will come the power to love and serve in a new, a diviner way.

To My Brother in Prison

Don't brand a man as a criminal. Teach him that he is a soul and give him a chance. Let him feel that

99

someone believes in him. Give him the encouragement that perhaps he has missed all through his life, and the lack of which may have helped to make him what he is.

I believe in the divinity of man. I believe that the potential god-life is within the murderer, the thief, the outcast, and that there lives no one who has it not. Why, then, do these types exist?

Because human nature is dual. In the life of the man who has made his mistakes we can see the forces of evil, the forces of the lower psychology, gradually taking control of that life until a certain point is reached — a climax; and then the man who is under their sway weakens and falls, in spite of his education, his intelligence or his wealth. Why? Because the subtle psychology of ignorance, selfish ambition or vice, has broken down and ruined the magnificent human system which is the temple of God.

If the hopeless, discouraged men in our prisons could be made to realize the potential strength of their higher natures, the latent spiritual force that lies within them waiting for the call, they would have the key to the problems of life.

100

Fear the criminal? Not I; he is labeled. It is the criminal who is not labeled whom we must look out for. We suffer more today from the class of wrong-doers who cloak themselves in hypocrisy and move among men unsuspected, than from the labeled class.

Aye, today I would rather trust myself in the hands of a murderer than in those of a hypocrite! And what discerning person would not?

❖

What a wonderful thing it would be if the nations could be so fired by the needs of those whom we call criminals that selfish and personal interests could be forgotten. Great convocations could be held in every city; mothers, fathers and children could gather together to work in consonance with that divine law which is ever ready to serve us. What an urge towards higher things humanity would receive from such an effort. Can you not believe that out of such great gatherings something new would arise? We should understand, to a degree at least, what Christ meant when he said to the woman who touched his garments, "What is this that hath gone out of me?"

101

That is what we must arouse — spiritual sympathy. We must arouse the mental and spiritual force of true compassion, to change the currents of retrogression that are now sweeping the best in our life away.

The secret of this work is sympathy with the souls of men.

Somewhere, somehow, at some time, we have failed in our duty or we should not have criminals in our midst. It is part of the divine law that we shall have just this result, however, until we awaken to our higher duty to our fellowmen.

The marvel is that with so little knowledge of their inner natures, of the dual forces that sway them now this way and now that, men do not go further astray. The marvel is, truly, that there is not more crime in the world, considering the obscurations on every hand in the mental life of man.

Criminals lose faith in humanity before they lose faith in themselves. Why is this the case? It is because so many declare them to be "sinners." They have made the gulf so wide between themselves and the so-called criminal classes that the latter make their own little world of criminality and become psychologized by it.

Let those who stand forth today as spiritual teachers, helpers of humanity, read their consciences, study their own natures. Then let them answer at the bar of justice as to why so many unfortunates drift into prison. And we, in the twentieth century, boasting of our civilization, support laws that consign them to the scaffold!

Let us pause and think for a moment. Let us imagine that *our* children were in prison today, that *our* children were to be executed! That is the way to bring home to ourselves the truth.

The thinking world today is quite ready to admit the influence of psychology; to admit that thoughts, in a sense, are things, and that the invisible, the intangible, the seemingly unexpressed, is sometimes the most potent in making or marring character. This has a great bearing upon questions of prison reform, for imprisoned men move and live, month after month and year after year, in a psychological atmosphere of condemnation and of gloom. Reminded that they are

103

outcasts, shut quite away from the world, forgotten and condemned, knowing only that the outside world is whirling on, moving on, *indifferent*, they learn to hate humanity for they have learned to hate themselves. They do not understand nor will they see that discipline is necessary and is best. They meet little, perhaps, that is sympathetic or compassionate — few signs indeed that we are our brother's keeper. This is not the case in every prison, but it is the case with the great majority.

The marvel to me is that these men do as well as they do, for they enter discouraged, and discouraged they come out. The very fact that so many really reform is to me proof of the divinity of man. And yet these men are our brothers, and sometime, somewhere along the way, we have done our part to encourage them in mistakes. We are pushing them into discouragement and crime even today by our indifference, our apathy, our selfishness, our unwillingness to admit that we have any duty towards them.

Let us look ahead ten or fifteen years and picture some of our hills and valleys presenting a new feature in twentieth-century civilization — a something that is splendidly remedial; and that is hospitals for the weaklings, the more unfortunate whose unbridled passions have carried them so far beyond the pale of society that prison walls close upon them.

There would be gardens and fields, and there would be houses and homes. I dare conceive a plan by which these prisoners should not be separated from their families. They should be cared for in such a way that they would understand quite well that they were under a certain restraint — but no more, perhaps, if we were very thoughtful, than we give to certain invalids. They would feel that they were in a hospital, in a school, with everything so helpful about them there would be no inducement to rebel.

I have had many years' experience in prison work, and I know that many of these unfortunates, possibly most of them, if properly encouraged and helped, would arouse the strength of their higher nature and in the course of time become valuable citizens, some of them, ultimately, lawmakers, teachers or reformers. How dare we say this could not be? How dare we stultify the possibilities of the soul of man? Can we not let the imagination soar as far as this into the broad arena of spiritual life?

If we can parole men now, leaving them with everything to contend with, no end of difficulties and everything to discourage, surely we could support a scheme of brotherhood reformatories, making them a universal expression of love from the hearts of the people, and limited by no special system except that of the laws of the state. I can feel your hearts pulsating with the thought of this picture.

One of our objects is to revive hope in the hearts of those who, through heredity or environment of a disadvantageous character, have suffered injustice. True brotherhood should have the quality of the sunlight; it should shine everywhere, irrespective of conditions. Its light should flash behind prison walls and bring a new feeling of life to those who are thus shut in through their mistakes. It ought to be remembered that the force misdirected by those in such unfortunate circumstances would, if properly applied, make heroes of them, and that under similar conditions many might be in the same position. Criticism and condemnation should give place to true love and compassion.

It is in the Law that we should instill into the hearts of the sorrowing and hopeless the mighty truths which

106

reveal the mysteries of life and of death. Picture that touch affecting the world. Picture the aching hearts in the prisons receiving the message not only in words but in that deeper way that words cannot express.

It is those who have passed through the chastening processes, the cleansing fires of suffering, who will gain spiritual knowledge *if they will but search for it*. It is they who will gain the real victory — the victory over the self. It is they who will be the forerunners of the new order; light-bringers for generations to come.

When we have more humane laws, when our prisons are used as educative and spiritualizing institutions, and when capital punishment is abolished, then and not until then can we look down the vistas of the future with the confidence born of clear vision and a sense of duty done.

And this is really the keynote — the recognition of the soul in men, whether they be black or white, despairing or hopeful. It is in all men.

It stands majestic, the core and heart of each man's life, the dictator of his destiny.

107

Keynotes and Epigrams

It is the inner life that man must bring forth. He must become a conscious part of universal law.

On human shoulders rests the responsibility for human progress.

The path of the mystic is a path of self-mastery and service.

Wherever the heart rules, spirituality is, for the heart is the seat of the soul.

To cater only to mental demands is to forge another link on lines of retrogression.

Selfishness is the line of greatest resistance. Why not choose the opposite and easy way?

Let us question ourselves and ask: are we doubters of, or believers in, the divine law?

We should adjust ourselves to fit like mosaic in the great plan of human life.

No man has a right to say he can do nothing for others.

No man is made happy by the mere possession of objects.

Let us make our every act the expression of all that is divinest in our hearts.

There must be heroic determination in our hearts for *continuity* of right action.

Evolution is the law of human life. All have evolved differently and each must shine according to his light.

Hypocrisy can have no place where one is trying to lead the theosophic life.

My aim is to make theosophy intensely practical, intensely serviceable.

The transition from mere intellectualism to practical, philanthropic activity was not effected without leaving behind a few who showed their theories to be but skin-deep.

The first step to be taken in occultism is the practice of unselfishness.

Selfishness is the basis of the world's unhappiness.

If the world is ever to become a better place, we must begin to think and act as divine souls.

Make each hour tell for some great mastery in character and in life.

The psychological mistakes of the past are still upon us. If we are to drink from the fountain of happiness we must learn to know the false from the true.

With all our experience we are as yet but touching the fringe of real life; we are but entering the outer portals of the real mysteries.

In studying the mysteries we are sitting at the feet of the higher law; we are opening the pages of the great book of human life.

Sympathy and toleration are required in every direction, for both are necessary to progress.

We are in soul-essence verily united. We cannot break that sacred tie.

We are weighed down as a people with the errors of the ages.

The secret of human life in its fullness is self-directed effort.

If we are to help humanity in a new way, we must begin to think in a new way.

Just as in studying music one has to place the voice, so in studying theosophy one has to place the mind; that is, one has to find the right mental attitude in order to understand.

A great hope is dawning for humanity. We seek to voice that hope.

Mental obscuration should not be your lot. Wisdom and light belong to you, for they are part of the heritage of man.

The surgeon's knife may hurt, but only that healing may come. So the teacher may wound at times, but only to the end that spiritual health may be established.

111

Waste no more time in argument. Find the SELF, and wrest from that the message it is waiting to impart.

When the heart is attuned to the sorrow and the needs of the world, the mind becomes illumined, and wisdom enters in. Those who possess the wisdom that is born of compassion, may truly be called inspired.

To tear down the life of another is but to destroy one's own.

Are you faultless? No, but you can strive towards faultlessness. Not your act but your motive is weighed in the scales of divine justice.

Prayer is aspiration, and true aspiration is prayer. The life that is lighted by it is a constant service of devotion, a burning altar-flame.

The Family and the Home

VI

To the Awakening Woman

THE world is starving for the psychological touch of something higher from women, and that something higher can spring only from an inner devotional attitude of mind. Without devotion we cannot be real women.

The devotional spirit ought to be more cultivated by women, for it opens a path to the soul. Men are waiting for it unconsciously, they are longing to see it manifest in women's lives, and when it is so manifest they feel it and respond to its appeal, even without a word being said. And our little children feel it also.

The devotional keynote in woman's life makes home a sacred place, for it sanctifies every hour of the day. When this wonderful spirit plays into and over the life, you are buoyed up, inspired: nothing is impossible; nothing is hard; nothing is too much. The wave carries you along, so to speak, and real magic is often the result. In depending solely on the intellectual life woman is starving herself, her children and her home, for she cannot convey to those who love her the heart-touch which their souls are calling for and should have.

It is the inner life, the heart-life, that woman must seek and strive to realize, with all the courage and soul-determination of her being.

I plead for the cultivation of the spiritual will that lies back of every heart and mind. I plead with woman to awaken to a realization of her divine potentiality to shape her own life and the lives of others to divine results. I plead with her to awaken to her mission in the world.

Woman, by nature, is mystical; she lives more in the heart. Her emotional nature, however, becomes a source of weakness if not governed understandingly. Could she harness and control that, new doors would open in her life continually; she would journey on an ever-ascending path of experience and spiritual growth.

The greatest work that woman can do today is to become so feminine, so spiritual and strong, so grandly compassionate and helpful, that she will hold the whole human family in her keeping. She will make the home her altar, her kingdom; and from that altar, from that kingdom, shall be sent out the gospel of life to all people.

We do not want any brain-mind work in such a reformation. My effort is to arouse your enthusiasm, to awaken in you a burning desire to know more of your real selves that you may better do your real duties. My effort is to evoke the inner and unrecognized part of you — the superb divinity within you, the soul — that you may step forth as positive, strong, royal examples of right action.

I have no receipts for you, no sentimentality, no crutches for you to lean upon. There is but one issue here, and it is this: shall the spiritual or the temporal woman rule? And my aim is to evoke from within you your own divinity, that something which will give you the power to overcome all difficulties. Once you have evoked this unconquerable power, which is yourself in very truth, you will find that half the difficulties in your life will have disappeared, and that the other half can be met with a courage so royal, so superb, that you can actually transform them into helps and victories.

117

I cannot conceive how we are ever to adjust and redeem humanity, or how we are ever to make the home an ideal place of love and harmony, until women understand themselves. For only when in possession of this priceless knowledge — the knowledge of the self — is it possible for either man or woman to develop and perfect that symmetry which is the ideal.

Woman has been slowly losing her way along the ages, beyond question — though the same may be said of man. But the obscurations and stumbling blocks in woman's path have been many and great and have brought into her life an unrest that few men realize.

I believe that men know very little about the inner life of woman, for unless man is acquainted with himself, with his essential divinity and his possibilities, how can he judge? On the other hand, if woman is unacquainted with herself, and in her turn knows not her essential divinity, how can she understand life, or duty? How can she become the ideal woman that her heart is pleading with her to be?

False education and the errors of ages have surrounded woman with environments that are unnatural

118

and unreal; and these in their turn have crippled her genius and forced her into a life that is not hers.

Woman must "know herself" for this is her true mission. She must unveil the mysteries of her being, and in the unveiling she will become transformed physically, mentally and spiritually, elevated to a higher expression of womanhood. She will no longer be limited to a small mental life, for her soul would not bear it. Her aspirations will be so high, her ideals so much higher, and her knowledge so much greater, that she will broaden her views, her life, her sphere of usefulness. Thus we should have not only the ideal woman, but the international woman. One nation would not be enough for her. She would hold the whole world in her love.

There is being enacted on the mental plane today a great battle in woman's life, a terrible struggle. It may not be written openly in history, but it is recorded in the atmosphere of the world and tells its story in the silence.

❖

If woman is to attain the dignity of ideal womanhood, she must cultivate her femininity. She was born

119

a woman and she must *be* a woman, in the truest sense. Contrasts between man and woman exist, yet there is a balance — the heart-yearnings perhaps different in each, yet both reaching towards the same goal; their intellectual life somewhat different, developed under different conditions and environments, yet this too reaching towards the same consummation and achievement.

These contrasts hold within themselves, in the deep undercurrents of human life, a superb and glorious harmony. Woman in her true place, hand in hand with man in his, would bring about a new order of things — a new life, a resurrection of the spirit, a shining forth of the inner, higher, eternal qualities of the human soul.

Both men and women come from the same divine source; they are seeking the same goal, are part of the same universal life, are guided by the same universal laws of being. Outward aspects are different in each, and duties are different; but the hunger for truth is the same in both, the spiritual will the same.

The first thing a woman has to learn, when she studies the laws governing her life, is that there is a negative and a positive quality in human nature, and that negative women are always imposed upon. They are forever sacrificing their lives to no beneficial result, forever bearing children in disharmony, who must later suffer just as they have done. For there is no balance in their lives; there is no justice.

On the other hand, when a woman begins to live the higher life, and live it positively, forcefully and fully, the very atmosphere of her presence silences the meanest and most selfish efforts of her opposers.

You cannot make over the world in a moment, nor can you change woman's life in a moment. Realizing the mistakes that have been made all down the ages, therefore, let woman become acquainted with herself. Let her not become so anxious to succeed, however, that she loses her balance, and let her above all remember that the crucifixions in human life have often proved to be its blessings.

Let the woman who finds herself unhappily married, or suffering from conditions brought about through marriage, remember that these things came about because she was not acquainted with herself. When the time for choice drew near, had she known how to accentuate in her life the positive quality, the power

121

of intuition — the great spiritual factor in life — would have illumined her mind. It would have brought to her a knowledge not only of her weakness but also of her strength.

In studying themselves men and women should first of all study their nature in its duality — the play and interplay of the higher and the lower self. This step taken, they should then search out their greatest weaknesses, as revealed in the light of such study, and courageously begin to overcome them. This initiates a great process of purification, and with a devotional attitude of mind behind the self-analysis, a double work is going on: an inner work and an outer.

We are too prone to rest content within the little limited circle of what we consider our necessities, and lose sight of the spiritual meaning of our lives. It is a common human failing.

How many can analyze themselves, or bring about a living unity between themselves and their life? Far too many live in their puny prejudices and their wants. "What I want" is the mantram of civilization at the present day — so rarely "what I need" or "what civilization demands."

122

THE FAMILY AND THE HOME

If you could only know what a companion the higher self can be! It is a presence, a mystic presence. The realization of it depends of course upon the degree of your evolution. Its companionship is so real, so wonderful, so royally supreme. Once you have found it, you never can lose it again.

Even among very diverse types of people the same thing is often lacking in each, namely, the strong spiritual will. This should be the moving power in every human being, but in most men and women, through lack of understanding and of exercise, it is too weak to amount to a real force in directing the life.

Until aroused to some understanding of the spiritual will and thus set upon the right track — which is that of self-directed evolution, spiritual self-reliance, in a word — we cannot know ourselves; nor can we realize who or what we are, or know what part we are to play in life. We cannot touch even the fringe of spiritual truth.

I believe that one of woman's greatest weaknesses is the fact that she does not discriminate, often, between true sympathy and false. And false sympathy is one of the greatest of all stumbling blocks in the soul's path — one's own path or that of another. To make this weak point strong, woman must study her nature *in its duality*, for without this knowledge one is often helpless to discriminate between the pull of the emotions, which disintegrate and exhaust, and the urge of true sympathy, which is supremely spiritual in its power.

Sympathy is always imaginative, bringing to us true pictures and true knowledge of the work of aid which lies before us. Sympathy makes human minds so plastic that words are hardly needed to find out the cause of another's trouble. Sympathy translates itself into action almost without the aid of human speech.

❖

The whole world seems to be going mad over "my rights," "my city's rights," "my country's rights." But what about *my duty?*

I hold that the injustice which is now so marked in human life is based on the misuse of these two words, "my rights." Absence of real unselfishness and of love for duty is so marked that duty as a fact and an ideal has not the place it should have in the hearts and minds of men.

We cannot have the illumination that comes from the higher self without being constantly devoted to duty. It is the most splendid companion we can conceive of — DUTY!

Women can no longer fold their hands and say, "I cannot touch unpleasant subjects; they do not concern me." Whatever menaces the purity of human life or the innocence of the youth concerns women deeply and must be touched upon by them, in thought and feeling both, before the outer reforms that the few are working to secure can be built upon a basis that is enduring.

I hold that if women were rightly placed today — or if they had rightly placed themselves, realizing their deeper potentialities, their divine possibilities, and their sacred mission — the world would not be so all awry. There would be real cooperation between women and men, a better understanding of each other's natures, and a new line of higher living for both. This must come about if the dream of world reconstruction is to be made a living fact.

But it is impossible and would be most unjust to say that woman is to be blamed, or that man must be.

It is the unnatural conditions in general human life today that too often hem women in and hold them down, causing unrest and consequent unhappiness. These conditions react upon man; the unrest thus created reacts in its turn upon woman, and the combined influence of their mutual unrest and doubt falls upon the children, the home – and the nation.

In endeavoring to urge upon women a profounder recognition of all that pertains to the unfolding of their higher natures, I hold that were a real effort to be made towards this end by men and women working together, the twentieth century would mark the beginning of a great spiritual uplift on absolutely new lines.

Build Spiritual Altars in the Home

Here is another problem: are the mothers and fathers, the educators and the progressive minds of the age, satisfied with the home life of today? Do we not realize that under the present outlook future generations can have little of the greater hope? Are not crimes increasing, crimes unspeakable? Are we not reaping, day by day, the harvest of our acts of omission in the past, our failure to make our home life what it should be, all along the way?

The question naturally arises: what can bring about a change for the better? What factors can be introduced that will readjust our home life *as nations* — for there are sublime exceptions in individual life — and bring it nearer to perfection?

Men and women should study the laws of life and the responsibilities of fatherhood and motherhood even before marriage. Home should be acclaimed as the center from which the higher life of the nations is to spring.

In this great reconstructive effort, the question is often asked: where shall we begin? But does not the home preeminently afford us opportunities for living the grander life? Can we not through the home bring more quickly than otherwise something new and uplifting into the world?

❖

Humanity needs health, physical, mental and moral; and children born under right conditions, physically strong and well, and spiritually in the atmosphere of the real harmonies of life, receptive to that light which was

127

shed upon the life under prenatal conditions — such as these cannot but become splendid vehicles for spiritual development, temples of the inner, living god. When the whole nature is in balance, there will be innate, not only tendencies towards the devotional life, but an intellectual aspiration for all that is high and noble.

Such children would grow day by day in spiritual life under the guidance of parents who had placed themselves in harmony with the higher law, and such parents, in their aspiration to serve their little ones and pass down to later ages a noble expression of childhood, manhood and womanhood, would be building not merely for the present but for all time. Perpetuating their ideals in their children, such home-builders would begin to make real the Kingdom of Heaven upon earth.

The charm and fascination of the picture lies in the fact that "the Kingdom of Heaven is within." Storms may be without, trials, poverty, struggles, tragedies, disappointments of all kinds; but however many they may be or however great their force, they cannot daunt. Within is heaven, reflected in that home — an expression of the higher law, the Christos-spirit, the life of the real man, the real woman, with woman in

128

her true place and man in his, as the higher law intended them to be.

I hold that the time is near when men and women shall declare true marriage to be a creation of the divine or higher law, and the bond of the civil law but a form for purposes of protection. Wherever a marriage exists, not sanctioned by this divine power, where souls are not united spiritually and filled with the highest ideals and the purest love, there is no real marriage at all.

With this conception as a guide, it could not be long before those who have the common interests of the world at heart would find new light and would live in accordance with their responsibilities.

One can touch upon the subject of marriage at present in only a fragmentary way. But there are profound mysteries connected with it, and could we study them rightly we could begin to build a new world.

I find myself so often moving back from the outer world into the inner world of the home, appealing in the silence to the mothers, daughters and wives to do their part more fully to bring about a new state of affairs. There is grave need of readjustment in the life of nations all over the world, and if women could take up this work in relation to the home life which they touch at one or another point — not selfishly, but in the interest of suffering humanity — the results would be more far-reaching than they dream. That done, the world would soon respond to the influence of a new psychology, the psychology of the higher self.

To build the nation righteously we must build our homes sacredly, and those who work towards that end should study the heart-doctrine and live it. There is need of more light for the people, but it cannot be found until the sacredness of fatherhood and motherhood, and the higher meaning of brotherhood, are better appreciated and understood.

Without knowledge we cannot live understandingly; if we are to serve our fellows we must *know ourselves* and we must know the laws of life, that we may build the home morally and spiritually, fashioning every thought and act in harmony with these laws.

However farfetched my statements may seem today, it will ere long be recognized by science that there exists a psychological force that is intangible and invisible yet stronger than words can paint. How carefully we guard our children against whooping cough and measles, and yet how thoughtlessly they are exposed to psychological influences which are a thousand times more fatal!

The human family is moving towards the realization of great truths, and in this connection we should commence to build on broader and more unselfish lines of effort; we should cultivate a divine courage, and we should begin in the home, with a sacred comprehension of the married state.

A true home is a light upon the pathway of the world's life. When the homes of the world are based on justice and a higher type of love we shall have no more disheartening national and international problems.

Child and Mother

I wonder how many parents think much about the real responsibilities of life, how many understand the real sacredness of marriage and that most sacred thing of all: the ushering of souls into the world!

131

Home is a great school of experience. It is the place of affection, the center where children should be born and reared in harmony with the higher law.

The currents of thought at work throughout the whole organism of humanity are registered on the minds of all as on a sensitive plate. In every country there are thousands concentrating their minds on the injustice under which they suffer, and in no way does this condition of things affect the world more deeply than by prenatal influence.

If in the case of an assassin, for example, we could trace the inner development of the nature, we might find the real cause for his crime in the little uncorrected mistakes of childhood, in seemingly unimportant habits, which grew and grew until they became a part of the very life.

The ultimate cause might even be found, could we go back to it, in an indifferent or careless thought on the part of the mother during the prenatal period of her child's life. The sins and crimes of the world are really commenced in the cradle.

132

It would be absurd to say that children are born in sin, for all are divine and birth is the door through which the immortal self enters to gain experience. But I do say that they can be, and often are, psychologized in weakness on the negative side of their natures, even before birth, by loving but unwise mothers.

Let your children learn to face real issues in their childhood. Let them be taught something besides the love of pleasure, love of the dollar and of ease. Let us bring home to them *new* lessons, for they are hungering for them; they are seeking the light; they are pleading all the time in their silent way for more knowledge. Is not your duty to them plain?

The personal desires that sometimes work insidiously in the minds of parents affect the rising generation. The narrow grooves of thought through which they often seek to lay down the law as to what occupations their children should follow, draw them away from the true purpose of their lives and hamper the expression of the divine principle within them.

There can be no question about the mother's love, but sometimes by this very means mistakes are made which affect the minds of the young so materially that their power for good becomes dwarfed. But when, without selfish ideas of personal advancement, the mother follows her intuition, the results on her family are vastly different.

When all these influences are considered, a point is reached where no further light is possible unless the idea of rebirth is understood. How differently parents would act if they fully realized that their little ones came "trailing clouds of glory" from a great past, traveling down the ages to the present time.

❖

Woman has it within her power to become a pillar of spiritual strength, and the great rising temple of humanity is waiting in the silence of things for just the support that she is so qualified to give. Shall she therefore step forth in the royal dignity of the higher self and take up the duty of the hour — or fail? She must do one or the other, for there is no possibility of standing still. Mighty currents of disintegration are sweeping into the heart-life of humanity at the present time, created by the prevailing spirit of unrest and in their turn creating more unrest, and those who will not enter the great divine currents of unselfishness and love will be swept down and away. Disintegration of character along most unexpected lines is one of the signs of the times. Yet the dawn of better things is near.

Keep the light burning in your hearts, and like watchers on the hills of peace you will see the first faint gleams of the new day ere you dream the day is at hand.

Ideals and the Child

VII

The Cycle of the Children

IT is impossible to gauge the significance of the present time or to realize what is in store for humanity during the next hundred years, merely from our own experience and from recorded history. For this is no ordinary time. It is not simply the culminating point of the past hundred years, but of thousands of years; the night of centuries has passed, and with the new dawn comes the return of memories and powers and possibilities of an age long past.

The soul of man still cries out, the darkness is still so close about him that he knows not the dawn is so near. But those who have climbed to the hilltops have seen the glow in the eastern sky and the rays of golden light in the heavens; and with the suddenness of the break of day in the tropics, in the twinkling of an eye, the light will come, the scales fall from our eyes, and we shall see — not in the uncertain gloom of night, but in the glorious sunlight.

139

As the light of day scatters the shadows and the powers of darkness, so will the effulgence of the new cycle break through the dark places of ignorance, prejudice and unbrotherliness in the age now so swiftly passing. The great heroes of old will once more return to earth, the great musicians, painters, poets, wise statesmen, lovers of the race, will again take up their loving task, and the earth shall blossom as a garden. The ancient wisdom taught in the sacred Mysteries will be revived; the earth, the air, the ether, all nature, will reveal their secrets to those who have prepared themselves through purification and by service to humanity.

Such is the outlook into the future. To measure it, go back to the glory of ancient Egypt and to the yet older civilization and vaster achievements of ancient America. Such a future awaits us and our children and, if we are faithful, shall be ours in the new time when, after a brief night of death, we return to take up our work again upon earth.

Our children are pleading with us in the silence for a higher manifestation of soul-life. Let us approach them in a new way — not merely as "the sweetest little things on earth, and all mine" — but as sacred charges entrusted to our care. And along this line let us refashion all our thoughts and acts. We must not merely *play* a part; we must *be* that part.

Are even the best home environments all that they should be? Do we not well know that nearly always there exist some conditions in the home that are adverse to the child's best interests? Children are imitators and carry a lasting impression of the knowledge gained, and the habits acquired, through home environment and example. It is idle for parents to attempt to teach their children self-control until they themselves have become examples of patience, firmness, poise and forbearance, until in *their* daily lives they are accentuating the virtues they preach to their children.

Children are often wiser than we know, often more observant than their elders. They are keenly receptive and responsive to what they hear, see and feel, either of good or evil. Intensely sensitive in their childish natures, they are much more affected by the mental atmosphere in which they live than is generally recognized. They suffer beyond description from discord and unhappiness in the home. They miss the inspiration which their hearts crave and which would come

141

from happy and harmonious surroundings. Many a boy and girl have gone the wrong way, unconscious of the results which would follow, because deprived of that tender, soul-nurturing care that belonged to them by right and which their parents should have given.

Our children may be the saviors of the world. Believing in reincarnation as I do, I know that they have returned to us with the sorrows of the ages written upon their hearts. Watch little children in their quiet moments; look into their innocent, wonderful eyes, and tell me if you cannot find more truth therein than in all the sermons you ever heard. And this is why I declare that just so far as we limit their knowledge of higher things, just so far as we hem them in mentally by dogmatic teaching, we are committing crimes.

❖

Cultivate a sense of spiritual honor in the child. Keep its mind filled with little duties, for idleness destroys soul-life.

The secret of happy childhood is not self-indulgence, however tempered and refined, but happy, wholesome, rational self-control.

142

Self-control! It can be taught to the babe in the cradle. It can be ingrained into character even before birth by the mother's own picture, kept constantly before her, of the ideal life; with her aspiration and her questionings all along the way: Who am I? Why am I here? What is my higher duty? Why must I strive for self-control?

Let the mother question thus and immediately there follows introspection: she begins to put her mental house in order. She goes back to her childhood in thought, perhaps, and comes to realize wherein lack of self-control has been the undoing of her nature, here and there and in one or another degree. The superb processes of self-analysis and introspection, inspired by pure motive and love for the child coming to her, must naturally bring that mother to a new state of consciousness. She has lighted her torch from the fires of divine knowledge; she has entered a new and a spiritual path, and you cannot hold her back. She has found the secret of new life.

And while she is so receptive — as she is at such a time, when the mysterious processes of the divine law are shaping the life that is to be, when the over-shadowing soul of her child is even then seeking recog-

143

nition — she finds herself another woman. She has become transfigured, transformed. And her child will not be fettered with her weaknesses, nor even with its own, for the mother has planted in its very being the secret of self-control. She has planted in the little mind, even before it has felt the sunshine, an insight and a power that will stay. Realizing her responsibility, and finding in a new way the power that is born of forbearance and of trust, she fashions for that little child a new house to live in, for she holds it in the atmosphere of the soul.

If we are to keep our children unspoiled and with simple and wholesome tastes, we must cultivate in them great refinement, love of order and cleanliness, and the spirit of obedience. Avoid repressing the child. Teach it that obedience is a loving expression of its better nature — not something blindly imposed upon it by force.

Certain hours of the day or evening should be kept regularly by parents in which to meet with their children, quite apart from other attractions, entertainments or duties. Parents should endeavor to create a spirit of true cooperation and mutual trust, that these hours may be times of mutual benefit. The real heart-nature of the child may thus be brought out at an early age.

Not until parents understand the duality of man's nature and his power to control any tendency to surrender to temptation, are they competent to establish rules of conduct for their children.

Education and the Heart-life of the Child

The secret of true education? It lies in the heart-life of the child.

Every essential moral lesson which can be taught to adults can be taught also to children; and surely it is better that the little ones should learn, in the love and sanctity of the home, the lessons which the world has a rougher method of imparting at an age when mental habits have become confirmed.

To teach the little children their divine nature, to impress this fact upon them, is to lay the cornerstone of a healthy, happy manhood and womanhood.

145

We must remember that early childhood opportunities are precious; that the character is more susceptible to the influence of thoughts and actions than in mature life; that the child's growth and happiness depend upon its yesterdays — its babyhood beginnings — and that the present must be used in rational and wise preparation for its tomorrows.

You may organize systems of thought, or found societies and associations for the betterment of humanity; but these can do little permanent good because there is lacking a universal system of education for the youth.

The world is tired, humanity is tired, of the merely intellectual life of the age. It is crying out for some clear manifestation of truth, some glowing, compassionate expression of the heart-life.

Enlightened education is not so much a something which is imparted. It is a liberation from the powers of the lower forces of the nature, which hinder and check a growth which ought to be unchecked and spontaneous.

146

We have been trained so long on lines of false education that our very blood is teeming with its poison. It is in the very atmosphere of our breathing life. It is all around us, and our brain-minds are so permeated with the false teachings of the age that we imagine it difficult to take up our simple possibilities, grand as they are, and to feel that we actually can have the spiritual knowledge that shall reveal all things — all the secrets of life.

True education is, in reality, a permission to the child to grow without the chains of self-love, which will ever remain outside of its nature if the foundations of education be laid aright. Are there not many parents who even admire in their children the faults which may, as adults, bring them within reach of the law — encouraging in them the self-will and the vanity which must surely mar their lives?

The world has not yet realized how much of truth children already know, and how much of that truth we destroy by our mistakes. There are few children who do not know that nature is a great teacher, until we, by our materialism, and often by our ridicule, drive the knowledge from their minds.

147

Let the lives of the little ones be molded so that they will be better citizens than you or I. Let us cultivate a higher spirit of patriotism, a deeper spirituality, a greater spirit of brotherly love.

Children should be taught to regard themselves as integral and responsible parts of the nation to which they belong. They should be taught to aspire to the position of national benefactors, teachers and helpers, and so to become exponents of the truest and wisest patriotism.

In the nurseries and schools of the world the principle of selfishness seems often to be exalted into a virtue. "Preparation for life" seems all too often to consist in the cultivation of those aspects of the nature which have already done so much to create the misery which we see. The habit of self-interest, the "duty" of competition, are taught from the earliest and most impressionable days by many who would be the last to work consciously and willfully to impede the child's real growth. And children so taught, being left in ignorance of their own nature, its complexities and its intricacies, are unable to discriminate between the higher self and the lower, between the true and the false in life.

148

When children are treated in accordance with the facts and the needs of life, the love which is given them is that truest affection which thinks ever of their welfare, without regard to the selfish pleasure which they can render in return. To love a child truly is to help it to develop its highest faculties, which grow by, and through, a willing service to others.

Our so-called spiritual education is too often confined to a single hour on one day in the week — a single hour once in seven days! Yet how few, even among the best and wisest of parents, feel it an obligation to separate themselves from other cares to train the spiritual will and direct the abounding energies of their children — so tied down are they by false standards. Yet when these children grow to manhood or womanhood we are horrified to see, if not in our immediate family then in the community, the inebriate, the suicide, the criminal, the spiritual failure.

This is not a pleasant picture, but we should not shrink from it if we can learn a useful lesson, and through the knowledge thus gained help the coming generations. I say this in no spirit of censure, believe me, for these mistakes are due in the main to the ignorance of the age, to false ideals in education,

149

and to the lower psychology upon which we have been feeding the mind of man for centuries.

I realized many years ago that something was vitally wrong with all our scheme of things — with our conventions, our reformatory efforts, our charities. In the very shadow of the churches I saw vice and suffering and want. Worse still, everywhere I saw people moving along the even tenor of their ways, blissfully oblivious or frankly indifferent.

Never could I reconcile myself to such a bland acceptance of things. I must at least try to ameliorate conditions. I saw hardship as the result of vice, and vice as the outcome of hardship. I realized that all of our systems of helpfulness were totally backhanded. We dealt then, as most people deal now, with effects rather than with causes. *After* the damage is done, we attempt to repair.

What I wanted to do was *to prevent* — to prevent the damage being done. The world was already fairly well equipped with havens for the beaten and the fallen. I wanted to evolve an institution that would take humanity in hand *before* it was worsted in the struggle of life.

150

The truest and grandest thing of all as regards
education is to attract the mind of the child to the
fact that the immortal self is ever seeking to bring
the whole being into a state of perfection. The real
secret is rather to evolve the child's character than to
overtax the child's mind; it is to bring *out* rather than
to bring *to* the faculties of the child. The grander part
is from within.

To do this no part can be neglected, and the physical nature must share to the full in the care and
attention which are required. Neither can the most
assiduous training of the intellect be passed over; it
must be made subservient, however, to the forces of
the heart. The intellect must be the servant, not the
master, if order and equilibrium are to be attained.
Hence, the aim and object of true education is the
perfect balance of all the faculties — physical, mental
and spiritual — in a word, CHARACTER.

Seeing that the children of today will be the men
and women of the future, the great importance of this
work surely cannot be overestimated. Only by wise
teaching, by training in self-reliance, self-discipline,
concentration, and a recognition of the power of
silence, can the lower qualities of the nature be over-

come and the higher developed. One of the great objectives must be to bring home to their minds the old, old teaching that they are immortal souls, not divorced from beneficent nature, but in deed and truth a part of it.

Music is the Song of the Soul

Music is one of the cornerstones of true education. The world has not yet awakened to its value as a factor in refining and purifying the character, especially during the early and more plastic years of life.

Man is essentially a creator, and he can be considered in no other way. Theosophy, therefore, as the science of the immortal man, is creative on the highest lines. It brings the soul into action, ennobles the nature, frees the mind and inspires, so that naturally it finds expression, directly and indirectly, in both art and music.

There is an immense correspondence between music on the one hand, and thought and aspiration on the

152

other, and only that deserves the name of music to which the noblest and purest aspirations are responsive.

One who really desires to understand the soul of things is ever careful in the selection of music, ever heedful as to what notes are sounded in the hearts of men, lest some great harm be done instead of good.

There is a science of consciousness, and into that science music can enter more largely than is usually supposed. A knowledge of the laws of life can be neither profound nor wide which thus neglects one of the most effective of all forces.

Let us bring our children, therefore, close to the refining influences of the best in art and music. In doing so, however, let us realize that the power of beautiful expression in these things is not an affair of the intellect alone, or of custom or convention. Nor can it be learned from books. It comes from the awakening of the inner powers of the soul, those qualities of the nature which are in sympathy with whatever is high and pure.

Music is the song of the soul, and well we know that it has not yet fulfilled its function. Had I the

153

millions that are yearly given out in charity, my first work after I had fed the hungry and clothed the naked, would be to give such help to the families of the poor as would lead to the establishment of a musical life in even the humblest household. For when the soul is stirred by music, when we feel ourselves within reach of the higher ideals of life, then we find the light. Do you not know how deeply we can be moved even by the old church hymns, in spite of the old-fashioned theology that pervades them?

❖

The world has a wrong conception of the ideal in music, and not until it has rectified this can it perceive that true harmony can never proceed from one who has not that harmony within himself.

Ideally, music should be a part of the daily life, not merely as an exercise which occupies its stated times and seasons, but as a principle which animates all the activities. The soul-power which is called forth by a harmony well delivered and well received does not die away with the conclusion of the piece. It has elicited a response from within the nature, the whole being has been keyed to a higher pitch of activity, and even the smallest of the daily duties, those which are usually called menial, will be performed in a different way.

As is the case with music, art is a principle which should pervade all life and activity, following faithfully upon the lines of the science of the soul. Under this science, the arts become the true expression of soul-ideals, and no longer adventitious or capricious additions to our environment, but integral parts of that to which they belong. They become in themselves the expression of the law of evolution, and the demonstration of the reality of that law.

Music! What wonderful power lies in it to swing us out into the universal life! To realize its power is to realize that when self is forgotten, when personalities disappear, we are free — out in the open air of thought and love and the higher purposes. And yet even the best that we have today is but a materialistic expression in comparison with what it will be. Everything in music is so imperfect as yet: we are but touching the fringe of the real harmony.

If we could hold ourselves in the attitude of mind that is created when true music touches us; if we could

155

bind and fasten ourselves to the larger views it opens out and broaden our comprehension of what life really means, we could tear down the veil that divides the seen from the unseen, the seeming from the real; we could look at life as it really is, at ourselves as we really are.

I have always believed that music should be a power among the masses; that the god of music should rule every household, and that the little children, indeed the whole family, should give as much attention to music as to the other *duties* in life. If that were only the case, what a beautiful world this would be! Were we only taught the simple, fundamental laws of music, we could throw ourselves upon our soul-resources when under the shadow of the sorrows and trials of life, and sing ourselves once more into harmony and usefulness, into the light and joy of life.

True Drama, the Soul's Interpreter

The drama, like music, is regarded by the world as one of the relaxations of life because it is supposed to deal with unrealities. True drama points away from

156

unrealities to the real life of the soul. As such the drama should lead and guide the public taste, providing it with ideals towards which it can aspire. Nowhere are the advantages of this more strikingly illustrated than in the dramatic power which can be called forth wherever there is an absence of self-consciousness and of vanity.

Nowhere in the social life of the present is the need for reform more manifest than in the drama. In too many directions it has been made to serve the sensationalism of the day and to stimulate the vicious thought which it might be so powerful to suppress.

We are within sight of the time which will restore the drama to its rightful position as one of the great redemptive forces of the age.

Dramatic study is one of the most important factors in the right education of the child, for true drama is the soul's interpreter, the great creative exponent of the spiritual life.

It is the heart that the drama reaches with its message. That is the secret of its power to regenerate.

157

Life so needs beauty and laughter! My aim in presenting this drama (*As You Like It*) is in part to bring these back. I would have you mirthful with me in the golden world pictured in this play. Wholesome mirth is creative in itself. Shakespeare brought back to us the spirit of ancient beauty.

Man cannot be preached into virtue nor forced into happiness. He must be led to love them through the heart-touch. Your higher drama is your real reformer.

The life which is inspired by hope is necessarily the life which is rich in achievement, and man does indeed possess to the fullest extent a dominion over nature, vast and unimaginable.

The inertia of custom and convention has been already broken, and the unrest of the world, at which so many look with distrust and apprehension, is but the movement of the ship with the incoming tide of a purer and better thought. Ideals have been thrown out into the world, and because they are spiritual ideals they have entered into the minds of men and have painted entrancing pictures of what the world would be if man were but master of himself and of it.

Those ideals will not die away until they have been realized, until they have given birth to other ideals which will illuminate forever the roadway of all future life, declaring the reality of a reign of peace on earth and of the god in man.